Jamaica

Jamaica

BY RUTH BJORKLUND

Enchantment of the World™
Second Series

CHILDREN'S PRESS®

An Imprint of Scholastic Inc.

New York   Toronto   London   Auckland   Sydney
Mexico City   New Delhi   Hong Kong
Danbury, Connecticut

Frontispiece: **Rafting on the Rio Grande**

Consultant: Sonjah Stanley-Niaah, PhD, Senior Lecturer, Institute of Caribbean Studies, University of the West Indies, Mona, Jamaica

Please note: All statistics are as up-to-date as possible at the time of publication.

Book production by The Design Lab

Library of Congress Cataloging-in-Publication Data
Bjorklund, Ruth.
  Jamaica / by Ruth Bjorklund.
      pages cm. — (Enchantment of the world)
  Includes bibliographical references and index.
  Audience: Grades 4–6.
  ISBN 978-0-531-21252-3 (library binding)
  1. Jamaica—Juvenile literature. 2. Jamaica—History—Juvenile literature. 3. Jamaica—
Civilization—Juvenile literature. I. Title.
  F1872.2.B58 2015
  972.92—dc23   2014031109

1 2 3 4 5 6 7 8 9 10 R 24 23 22 21 20 19 18 17 16 15

Papaya tree

Contents

Left to right: **Family, Martha Brae River, friends, harvesting, fruit stand**

CHAPTER 1

Strong Roots, New Branches

IN LATE AUGUST, AFTER NEARLY THREE MONTHS AWAY from school, Delton prepared for a new year of classes. The summer had been a good one. Delton and his parents live just a block away from his grandparents in St. Ann, a farming community in the mountains of northern Jamaica, the third-largest island in the Caribbean Sea. Jamaican families keep close ties. Throughout the summer, Delton's city-dwelling aunts, uncles, and cousins visit often.

St. Ann is cooler in the summer than Kingston, the capital city where many of Delton's extended family lives. Breezes blow up from the ocean, and the mountains are lush with vegetation. Colorful tropical and migratory birds live in the trees, and many animals live near the cool, sparkling rivers and tumbling waterfalls. At night, Jamaican singing frogs fill the forest with thunderous song. Delton's cousins laugh and say the frogs are much louder than any ambulance siren or honking car they hear in the city.

Opposite: **A father and daughter relax on the beach in Ocho Rios, on the northern Jamaica coast. The average Jamaican family has two children.**

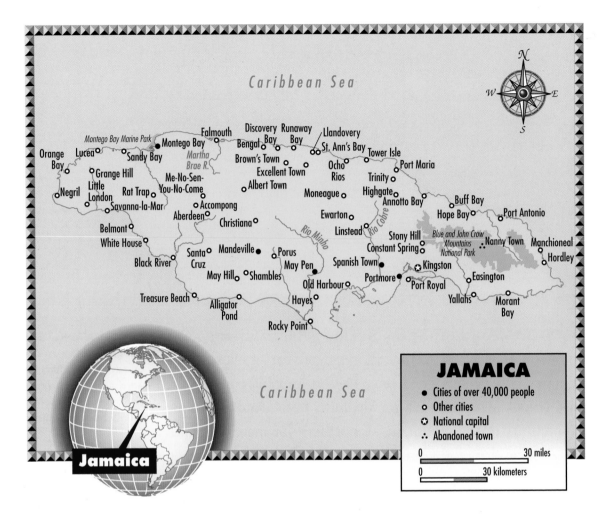

The map shows Jamaica with labeled locations including:

Caribbean Sea

Montego Bay Marine Park, Orange Bay, Lucea, Sandy Bay, Falmouth, Bengal, Discovery Bay, Runaway Bay, Llandovery, St. Ann's Bay, Tower Isle, Port Maria, Martha Brae R., Brown's Town, Grange Hill, Little London, Negril, Rat Trap, Me-No-Sen-You-No-Come, Excellent Town, Ocho Rios, Trinity, Highgate, Annotto Bay, Buff Bay, Port Antonio, Albert Town, Moneague, Savanna-la-Mar, Accompong, Aberdeen, Christiana, Ewarton, Linstead, Hope Bay, Nanny Town, Manchioneal, Belmont, White House, Santa Cruz, Mandeville, Porus, May Pen, Stony Hill, Constant Spring, Blue and John Crow Mountains National Park, Hordley, Black River, May Hill, Shambles, Spanish Town, Kingston, Easington, Treasure Beach, Alligator Pond, Hayes, Old Harbour, Portmore, Port Royal, Yallahs, Morant Bay, Rocky Point, Rio Minho, Rio Cobre

JAMAICA
- Cities of over 40,000 people
- Other cities
- National capital
- Abandoned town

0 ——— 30 miles
0 ——— 30 kilometers

Jamaica

To Market

Delton's parents are farmers. Like their neighbors, they tend a large household garden of vegetables and fruits, such as peas, yams, bananas, coconuts, and oranges. Delton's family grows pimento, a spice that is one of the country's most important agricultural exports, to sell at the market. The pimento tree is indigenous, or native, to Jamaica. Its berries are flavorful and aromatic. Pimento is a key ingredient in Jamaica's most famous dish, a spicy, sweet fire-roasted chicken called jerk.

Europeans first discovered pimento around 1500, a few years after Italian explorer Christopher Columbus landed in Jamaica and the Spanish established a colony there. Jamaica later became an English colony, and pimento became a sought-after British import.

Jamaican agriculture developed and became profitable because of slave labor. By the middle of the seventeenth century, Jamaica was home to an estimated seven thousand white colonists and forty thousand enslaved Africans. Like the majority of Jamaicans, Delton's ancestors were enslaved. For more than three hundred years, enslaved workers labored on plantations growing pimento, sugarcane, cacao, bananas, and

Jamaican women carry bananas to be packaged for shipping.

coffee. After slavery was finally abolished in Jamaica in the 1830s, Delton's family continued to work on a pimento plantation and saved enough money to buy a small farm of its own.

In a Jamaican family, no one is too young to contribute. Jamaican children are expected to perform chores. Chief among Delton's responsibilities is helping his parents prepare pimentos for sale and helping his mother weigh and package pimento leaves and berries for customers on market day. Throughout Jamaica, market day is held once a week. Market day is a colorful, noisy community event where farmers and merchants set up stalls to sell their fruits, vegetables, crafts, and supplies. The atmosphere is festive as musicians perform

Many kinds of vegetables are for sale at Jamaica's weekly markets.

on street corners while throngs of buyers circulate. Sellers called "higglers" appeal to their customers by shouting about the high quality and low cost of their products. Market day is a tradition that dates back to the time of slavery, when once a week, usually Sunday, slaves were allowed to set up outdoor markets and sell goods to one another.

A Jamaican man ties his boat down in preparation for the arrival of a hurricane.

Storm Watch

Although summer is a time that Delton can take a break from his studies and enjoy the company of his cousins, it can also be a time of loss because of the destructive tropical storms that sometimes blow through. Tropical storms bring violent winds, heavy rain, lightning, and damaging waves. Storms with winds over 75 miles per hour (120 kilometers per hour) are categorized as hurricanes. Some hurricanes have reached more than 150 miles per hour (240 kph).

A young man climbs a palm tree to harvest coconuts. The average coconut weighs about 3 pounds (1.3 kilograms), so it can be damaging when it falls.

The Jamaican government keeps watch on developing tropical storm patterns and warns citizens when a dangerous storm might make landfall. There are many ways citizens prepare, and Delton and other children have learned what to do. Delton helps his mother gather supplies such as canned food, fresh water, batteries, blankets, and flashlights. He fills the bathtub with water and carries inside the chairs and tables from the porch and lawn. Delton helps his father pick coconuts and mangoes because many injuries come from heavy fruit falling. They also pick bananas and oranges, whether they are ripe or not. They rush to harvest as much of the pimento as they can. Delton and his family have a plan to evacuate if their house is in danger. If they become separated, Delton will meet his parents in the basement of their church.

In October 2012, the Jamaican government issued a tropical storm warning while Delton was in school. Delton and his classmates were told to leave the school quickly. The warning said to prepare for the worst. The storm had gathered enormous force and had become a hurricane. On October 24, 2012, Hurricane Sandy struck Jamaica and devastated much of the island. Trees were ripped from the ground, roofs flew off buildings, windows broke, houses collapsed, cars were smashed, many people were injured and some were killed, and countless birds and animals were also killed. Farmers suffered horrible losses. All of Delton's family's pimento trees were stripped bare of leaves and fruit, and many lay uprooted.

Hurricane Sandy made landfall near Kingston. The storm caused US$100 million worth of damage in Jamaica.

Coming Together

After the storm, floodwaters coursed over the land. Most of Jamaica was without electricity for weeks. People living in impoverished towns and neighborhoods suffered the most because their poorly constructed homes could not withstand the storm. Food, water, and fuel were scarce around the country. But communities all over the island banded together to help one another. People who had fared better than others, such as Delton's family, welcomed the less fortunate into their homes and gave them food, comfort, and a dry place to sleep.

In Jamaica, Hurricane Sandy uprooted trees and ripped roofs off houses. About 70 percent of Jamaicans lost electricity during the storm.

Delton's parents and grandparents praised Delton for his hard work in preparing for the storm and his helpfulness afterward.

Over hundreds of years, Jamaicans have borne hardship with dignity, fellowship, and perseverance. The recovery from Hurricane Sandy was just one more example of Jamaican resilience and community spirit. Delton was proud to have had an important role in keeping his family and their home safe. After the hurricane, he joined his neighbors in helping make repairs and cleaning yards. In time, the farms in St. Ann began to heal. After five weeks, new leaves sprouted on the pimento trees. Birds and animals that had survived the storm reappeared, and the sound of Jamaican singing frogs echoed again in the night.

Men in Kingston move damaged trees in the aftermath of Hurricane Sandy. The storm caused extensive damage in eastern Jamaica.

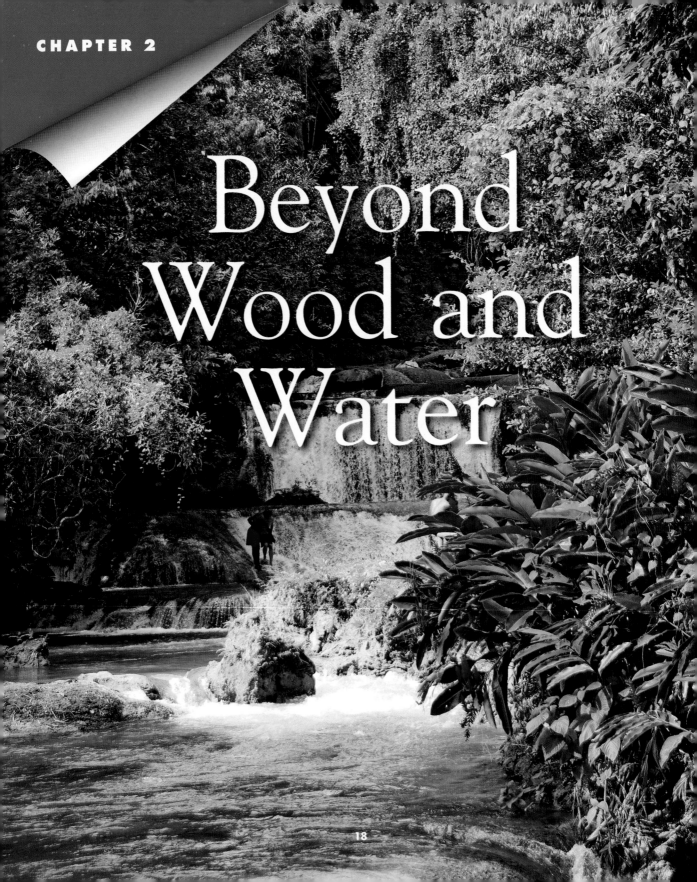

CHAPTER 2

Beyond Wood and Water

T HE PEOPLE OF THE TAINO CULTURE WERE THE FIRST to settle in Jamaica. They called the island Xaymaca, meaning the "land of wood and water." But the diversity of Jamaica is more than simply wood and water. It is a land of dramatic mountain ranges, tumbling waterfalls, rivers, swamps, forests, plains, caves, and beaches, all surrounded by the glistening waters of the Caribbean Sea.

Opposite: **Jamaica is renowned for its lush plant life and refreshing waterfalls.**

An Island and More

The island of Jamaica makes up most, but not all, of the nation of Jamaica. The nation is actually an archipelago, that is, a series of islands. Jamaica, by far the largest island in the group, lies to the north of a string of tiny uninhabited islands. Mainland Jamaica covers approximately 4,243 square miles (10,990 square kilometers), making it about half the size of the U.S. state of New Jersey.

Caribbean Basin

Encircling the archipelago is the Caribbean Sea, a part of the Atlantic Ocean that extends from the northern coast of South America to just south of the Gulf of Mexico. Jamaica lies approximately 580 miles (930 km) southeast of Miami, Florida, and 840 miles (1,350 km) northwest of Caracas, Venezuela. Its nearest Caribbean neighbor is the island nation of Cuba, 90 miles (145 km) to the north.

Mountain and Coast

The interior of the island of Jamaica is mountainous. The mountains run in an east–west direction, beginning gradually and rising up to Blue Mountain Peak, the highest point on the island, with an elevation of 7,402 feet (2,256 meters). The largest ranges in the east are the Blue and the John Crow Mountains. The mountains are separated by a deep gorge carved out by the Rio Grande River.

Jamaica's Geographic Features

Area: 4,243 square miles (10,990 sq km)

Highest Elevation: Blue Mountain Peak (right), 7,402 feet (2,256 m)

Lowest Elevation: Sea level, along the coasts

Greatest Distance East–West: 143 miles (230 km)

Greatest Distance North–South: 51 miles (82 km)

Longest River: Rio Minho 58 miles (93 km)

Average High Temperature: In Kingston, 87°F (30°C) in January; 91°F (33°C) in July

Average Low Temperature: In Kingston, 70°F (21°C) in January, 76°F (24°C) in July

Average Annual Rainfall: In Kingston, 32 inches (81 cm)

Greatest Average Annual Precipitation: Eastern Blue Mountains, about 300 inches (760 cm)

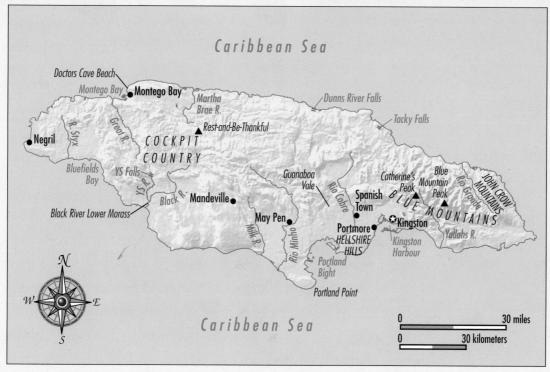

Creating Karst

The mountains that make up Jamaica and its island neighbors were formed by volcanic eruptions between 140 and 60 million years ago. Over time, the mountains eroded, and the sea eventually covered them. Jamaica and the other islands lay underwater. Then, about 13 million years ago, the land beneath the sea shifted and pushed the islands of the Caribbean up above the waves.

On the western side of Jamaica, the mountains are formed from sedimentary rock, a mixture of rock, lava, minerals, and organisms packed down over time. On the eastern side of the island, skeletons of sea life collected on top of the lava and rock, and hardened to form limestone. Rainwater becomes slightly acidic when it seeps through soil, which can cause the limestone to crack. As the cracks fill with more water, the limestone dissolves or wears away, creating the island's caves and pits, known as cockpits. This type of limestone is known as karst.

One of the most dramatic landforms in Jamaica lies in the central part of the island. The Cockpit Country is an eroded landscape called karst. In this region, water from rainfall, rivers, and underground streams has carved caves, pits (called cockpits), and sinkholes. Sharp limestone ridges separate one cockpit from another. Some of the cockpits are 400 feet (120 m) deep. The Cockpit Country contains the island's largest remaining rain forest.

The coastline of Jamaica is varied. The northeast shore, which is exposed to more wind and storms, is eroded and lined with rocky bays and inlets. In the north, there are calmer winds and waves, and narrow white sand beaches. A coral reef, an underwater ecosystem that supports a wide variety of life, lies offshore. The western coast has additional coral reefs and wide white sand beaches. Negril boasts a 10-mile-long (16 km) stretch of white sandy coastline. Many people consider it the nation's best beach.

The southwest coastline is a large, broad plain that extends several miles inland and is marked by rivers and swamps. The southern coast has several small black sand beaches at the base of steep limestone cliffs.

Many Rivers to Cross

More than one hundred rivers flow through Jamaica. Some rivers run underground, while others exist only during the

A boat travels along the lower Black River.

rainy season. Many others are fed by headwaters high in the mountains. The nation's longest river is the Rio Minho and its widest is the Black River. Other important rivers include the Martha Brae, the Rio Cobre, and the Great River. Many of the rivers flow down from the mountains to the sea at a roaring pace, creating deep riverbeds and waterfalls. Major waterfalls include the 600-foot-long (180 m) Dunns River Falls, the pristine and remote Tacky Falls, and YS Falls, a breathtaking waterfall that drops a total of 120 feet (37 m), cascading in and out of seven large pools.

Dunns River flows down a series of natural stairs, forming the Dunns River Falls, one of the most popular attractions in Jamaica.

The Black River begins underground in the Cockpit Country and resurfaces in the broad southern plains. Crossing the plains on its course to the sea, the Black River is joined by other rivers, including the YS River, to create a vast wetland region called the Black River Lower Morass. Covering almost 125 square miles (324 sq km), the wetland includes lagoons, limestone islands, marshes, and mudflats.

Warm Days

In Jamaica, temperatures are warm throughout the year. The average daytime temperature in July is 81 degrees Fahrenheit (27 degrees Celsius) and in January it is 76°F (24°C). At night, temperatures drop about 10 to 20 degrees Fahrenheit (6 to 11 degrees Celsius).

Clouds often collect in the Blue Mountains. More than 300 inches (760 cm) of rain falls annually in some parts of the mountain range.

Near the end of April, currents and winds drive tropical storms east to west, often along Jamaica's northern coast. This is the beginning of the hotter months, with high humidity, thunderstorms, and heavy rainfall. This is also hurricane season. One of these severe storms hits Jamaica every seven to eight years on average, bringing flooding, downed trees, and damaged buildings. The rainy season usually ends by November. In the winter months, the air is less humid, the winds are calmer, and less rain falls. Rainstorms that pass through affect the eastern mountain areas most. Much of the year, a blue mist hovers over the Blue Mountains, and sometimes in winter the peaks are covered in frost. The northeastern mountains also hold back rain clouds moving in from the east, leaving the plains on the other side of the mountains dry and reducing the region's rivers to a trickle.

Island Cities

The capital city of Kingston is the largest city in Jamaica, with a population of 666,041 in 2011. Its nearby suburb of Portmore is the second-largest city, home to 182,153 people.

Spanish Town, Jamaica's third-largest city with a population of 147,152, is the site of Jamaica's first capital. The Spanish chose the village of Villa de la Vega to be the capital in 1534. The town lies along the coast and was frequently raided by British pirates. In 1655, the English destroyed the town, renamed it Spanish Town, and made it their capital. Spanish Town served as Jamaica's capital for another 217 years and is home to many historic buildings (below). One of the most magnificent is the Spanish Town Cathedral. The church has a massive eight-sided spire with African faces carved into the stone. It was erected on top of the remains of Jamaica's first church, the Chapel of the Red Cross, built in 1525. Another important attraction is the People's Museum of Craft and Technology, which exhibits sugar and coffee plantation tools and machinery from the colonial era, artifacts related to slavery, and examples of traditional crafts.

Montego Bay is Jamaica's fourth-largest city, home to 110,115 people. Visitors to Jamaica often arrive via Montego Bay, a major port city on the northwestern coast. The city is a center for much of Jamaica's resort and tourist activities. In the city center, two historical structures honor Jamaican abolitionist heroes who fought to end slavery. Sam Sharpe Square commemorates Samuel Sharpe (above), an enslaved preacher who led a slave uprising called the Christmas Rebellion. Nearby, the Burchell Baptist Church honors Thomas Burchell, a white missionary who supported ending slavery. The city is also home to the Montego Bay Marine Park, which is renowned for its coral reefs that attract divers and snorkelers from near and far.

CHAPTER 3

Island in the Sun

A WIDE VARIETY OF PLANTS AND ANIMALS THRIVE in Jamaica's warm, wet climate. In 1687, British physician and avid botanist Hans Sloane traveled to Jamaica. When he arrived, he was stunned by the island's magnificent plants, fish, birds, and animals. He quickly began to record all the "herbs and trees and four-footed beasts" that he saw. Today, most of the species of plants and animals Sloane described still exist in Jamaica, and several are endemic, meaning they are found nowhere else in the world. These include Jamaica's national bird, a hummingbird called the red-billed streamertail, or doctor bird.

Living in Air

Bird-watchers come from all over the world to see Jamaica's spectacular array of birds. More than three hundred bird species can be found there. Some live on the island year-round, some migrate to the island during the winter months, and twenty-eight are endemic. In addition to the red-billed streamertail hummingbird, Jamaica's endemic birds include parrots called

Opposite: **The yellow-billed Amazon parrot often lives in damp forests, where it nests in large trees.**

Island in the Sun   **29**

the yellow-billed Amazon and the black-billed Amazon as well as the Jamaican lizard cuckoo. Two commonly seen birds are the Jamaican tody and Jamaican mockingbird. The tody is a mere 3 inches (8 centimeters) long, with a bright green body and red and yellow on its throat and chest. It nests in mud or rotten wood and lives on insects and fruit. The mockingbird, true to its name, repeats the songs of other birds, insects, and even frogs. A mockingbird can know as many as two hundred animal sounds. Jamaicans have many nicknames for their birds.

More than one hundred species of butterflies live in Jamaica, and twenty-one of them are endemic. The endemic Jamaican giant swallowtail butterfly is one of the largest butterfly species in the Western Hemisphere, with a wingspan of 6 inches (15 cm). The Jamaican giant swallowtail is unusual among butterflies in that it has a special organ behind its head

Doctor Bird

The Jamaica streamertail hummingbird is the national bird of Jamaica. The male hummingbird is colorful, with a black crest, iridescent feathers, and a long, two-pronged tail more than twice the length of its body. In Jamaica, the streamertail hummingbird is called the doctor bird. Some say this is because its crest and tail resemble the type of hat and coat a doctor historically wore. Others think the term came from the way the bird uses its bill to prick at flowers for their nectar like a doctor uses a needle. Legend has it that the Tainos, the people who first inhabited Jamaica, believed the bird had magical powers, so they called it the "god-bird."

when it is in its caterpillar stage. If a predator comes near the caterpillar, the organ secretes a foul odor. The butterfly is found only in remote areas, such as the Cockpit Country and the rain forests of the Blue and John Crow Mountains.

Mongooses tend to live alone and are active during the day.

The Four-Footed Beasts

Few land mammals live in Jamaica, but most of those that do were introduced by Europeans who brought dogs, cats, horses, goats, and cattle with them. The island has wild pigs, but they are not native. In 1872, the British introduced a small rodent, called the Indian mongoose, to rid sugarcane fields of rats. The mongoose saved many crops but it also devoured birds, reptiles, and amphibians and caused at least ten native species to go extinct. Today, the mongoose remains an unwanted pest that preys on animals.

Among the mammals native to Jamaica are twenty-two species of bats, including the Jamaican fig-eating bat and the Jamaican big free-tailed bat. The only endemic mammal is the Jamaican hutia, also called a mountain rabbit or coney. The hutia is a dark-haired rodent that resembles a guinea pig, with a large head and short ears and legs. It comes out only at night to feed on plants and fruits. The hutia is threatened because of habitat destruction, hunting, and mongoose attacks.

Ripples in the Water

Coral reefs line Jamaica's north shore and parts of its south shore. Corals are tiny, colorful animals related to jellyfish. They build a hard shell around themselves and attach to other corals, forming a colony, or reef. Corals are stationary. They feed on food floating past them by reaching out with their tentacles. Plants, sea grasses, and algae grow near the reef. In Jamaica, more than 250 species of fish live in the reef habitat. Small fish hide in the nooks formed in the reef and feed on plants and small marine life. Many reef fish are colorful, such as damselfish, rainbow parrotfish, and squirrel fish. Larger fish swim along the reef to feed on plants and smaller fish. Eels, seahorses, anemones, lobsters, sponges, and nurse sharks are also found in the coral reefs. Farther offshore live large fish such as marlin, barracuda, tuna, sailfish, and wahoo.

A few large marine mammals live in Jamaica. Some minke and humpback whales spend the winter in Jamaican waters before migrating north, while the sei and the short-finned pilot whale can be found in the region year-round. Three species of dolphins also live in the area throughout the year. The number of bottlenose dolphins in Jamaica has declined because they are often captured and used by resort owners as tourist attractions.

The Jamaican manatee is a large marine mammal that can grow up to 13 feet (4 m) long and weigh 1,200 pounds (544 kilograms). Despite their size, manatees are graceful and shy. Sometimes called a sea cow, the manatee is a distant cousin to the elephant. It has a large head with wrinkles and whiskers, a paddle-shaped tail, and two forearms called flippers. Jamaican manatees live in shallow rivers, marshes, and swamps. They eat mostly sea grasses and consume 10 to 15 percent of their body weight each day.

Manatees can stay underwater for about fifteen minutes before having to surface for air.

Reptiles and Amphibians

Jamaica is home to a wide variety of reptiles and amphibians. Many are endemic, including all nine species of snakes. No snakes in Jamaica are poisonous, though many people are afraid of the Jamaican boa, which can grow to 7 feet (2 m) in length.

More than two-dozen types of lizards live on the island, including anoles, geckos, skinks, and iguanas. The Jamaican anole is bright green, but changes colors to tan or brown to camouflage itself when hunting for food. The Jamaican croaking lizard is a type of gecko that lives in trees. Geckos often croak loudly in a chorus with other geckos. They can run straight up vertical surfaces and walk on surfaces upside down.

Race to the Sea

Some of the most threatened creatures in the world are sea turtles. Four species of these reptiles live in the warm waters off Jamaica: the hawksbill, loggerhead, green turtle, and leatherback. Sea turtles can live up to eighty years and weigh 350 pounds (159 kg). Female sea turtles return to the place of their birth to lay their eggs. Between May and December, they come ashore, dig nests in the sand, and lay dozens of eggs.

After hatching, the baby turtles scramble to the surface and begin their trek from nest to sea. They wait until sunset to avoid predator birds and crabs. Only one in one thousand hatchlings lives to adulthood.

Sea turtles were long hunted for their eggs and meat. Additionally, hawksbill sea turtles are prized for their beautiful patterned shells, which have been used to make jewelry and other items. The population of hawksbill sea turtles has been reduced by 90 percent in just one hundred years and the animal is now considered critically endangered. Jamaican scientists, international environmentalists, and local volunteers are organizing conservation programs to help sea turtles survive in the Caribbean.

Back from the Brink

The Jamaican iguana is the country's largest lizard and land animal, sometimes growing more than 5 feet (1.5 m) long. Once common throughout the country, the iguana was in steep decline by the late 1800s because mongooses, which had been brought in to control the rat and snake populations, also ate iguana eggs and babies. By 1948, the Jamaican iguana was thought to be extinct. But in 1990, a pig hunter found a small group of Jamaican iguanas living in the dry Hellshire Hills south of Kingston. The iguanas' eggs were brought back to the Hope Zoo in Kingston so the iguanas could hatch safely. Once the young iguanas were old enough to survive on their own, they were returned to the wild. Jamaican iguanas are now protected by law. The Hope Zoo is continuing its program of protecting eggs and hatchlings until the Jamaican iguana is no longer endangered.

Jamaica is also home to crocodiles, which live in wetlands. Unlike many crocodiles found around the world, Jamaican crocodiles are shy. They are also a threatened species because human development is damaging their wetland habitat.

At least twenty frog species are unique to Jamaica. Among them are the cockpit frog, the Jamaican red-eyed frog, the Jamaican laughing tree frog, and the Jamaican snoring frog. Jamaican frog species do not have a tadpole stage. Instead, the females lay their eggs in damp areas under rocks or rotting vegetation. Male frogs guard the eggs from predators, such as snails, birds, and snakes. When the frogs hatch, they look like miniature versions of their parents.

National Symbols

In a nation where hundreds of species of brilliantly colored flowers bloom, it is the less showy flower (right) from the guaiacum tree that is the national flower. The tree is also called lignum vitae, meaning "Wood of Life."

Tainos valued the tree for medicinal purposes. The Spanish and British discovered that the hardwood was excellent for building ship parts and tools.

The national tree of Jamaica is the blue mahoe, a fast-growing tree with broad leaves, feathery red flowers, and streaks of blue and yellow in the wood.

The national fruit of Jamaica is the ackee. Brought to Jamaica from West Africa in the 1700s, the ackee became an important part of Caribbean cuisine. The fruit has three black seeds and yellow flesh surrounded by a green skin. When ripe, the skin turns red and breaks open. If ackee is eaten unripe, it is poisonous.

Plant life

Jamaica is a host to more than three thousand different plants, trees, flowers, ferns, and grasses. Native trees include allspice, wild lime, cedar, Jamaican dogwood, and coconut palm. Bamboo forests grow in wet regions. Jamaican bamboo flowers only once every thirty to forty years. The nation boasts more than five hundred species of flowering plants and colorful, sweet-smelling orchids. The more remote regions of the island, including the Cockpit Country and the Blue and John Crow Mountains, have the greatest variety of plants. Elsewhere, forests have been logged and replaced with farms, homes, and businesses.

Some parts of the Jamaican coast are home to important habitats called mangrove swamps. Mangrove trees grow in

shallow tidal waters from a tangle of roots that rises from the muddy land. When the tide comes in, the mangrove roots are swamped. When the tide goes out, the roots collect mud and debris, gradually forming land. The roots also filter impurities out of the water. Mangrove swamps form a barrier that protects shorelines from storms. They also provide a habitat rich in nutrients for plant and marine life.

More than two hundred species of fish feed and shelter among the roots in Jamaica's mangrove forests.

Lush Land

The Blue and John Crow Mountains National Park was established in 1992 near the eastern end of the island. Today, the park contains the most lush and pristine parts of the island. The park is home to many rare species, including all of the island's endemic birds, the giant swallowtail butterfly, and the hutia. Hikers enjoy the many trails in the valley that separates the two mountain ranges. This region is thick with plants and has many waterfalls. A trail also leads to the top of Blue Mountain Peak. The peak is often shrouded in mist, but on a clear day hikers can see all the way to the island of Cuba, 90 miles (145 km) away.

CHAPTER 4

Turbulent History

HUMANS FIRST CAME ASHORE IN JAMAICA AROUND
600 CE. The Taino people, who belonged to a larger group called
the Arawaks, came from what is now Venezuela and established
settlements throughout the island. They caught fish, gathered
fruits, and farmed cassava, maize (corn), and yams. The Tainos
also gathered wild cotton and dyed it to weave brightly colored
hammocks. They crafted pottery, utensils, ceremonial objects,
and tools, and carved oceangoing canoes.

Opposite: **A scientist searches for artifacts at an ancient Taino site in southern Jamaica.**

Enter the Europeans

In 1494, Taino villagers living in what is now known
as Discovery Bay encountered Christopher Columbus, an
explorer for Spain, and his crew. Cautious at first, the Tainos
treated the newcomers with generosity. Columbus claimed
the island for Spain and named it St. Jago. Ten years later,
on Columbus's fourth voyage to the Caribbean, his ship was
damaged in a heavy storm and he and his crew spent a year in
Jamaica waiting for rescue.

In the years that followed, the relationship between the Spaniards and the Tainos took a downward turn. Spanish explorers wanted to find gold in the region. So in 1510, Columbus's son Diego led the first Spanish colonists into Jamaica. The first colony, Sevilla la Nueva (New Seville), was established on the northern coast near what is now St. Ann's Bay. This colony was not successful. There was little gold to be found, and most of it the Spanish simply stole from the Tainos. Villa de la Vega, the colony on the south side of the island, fared little better. The Spaniards used it mainly as a port to ship provisions to their other colonies. The Spaniards had introduced new crops to the island—sugarcane, citrus fruit, and bananas—and forced the Tainos to work as slaves on the farms. The Spanish also unwittingly infected the Taino people with deadly European diseases. By the mid-1600s, the combined forces of disease, overwork, and brutality had devastated the Taino population. Without the free labor of enslaved Tainos, Spanish plantation owners began buying enslaved Africans. But the colonists did not prosper, and many left the island.

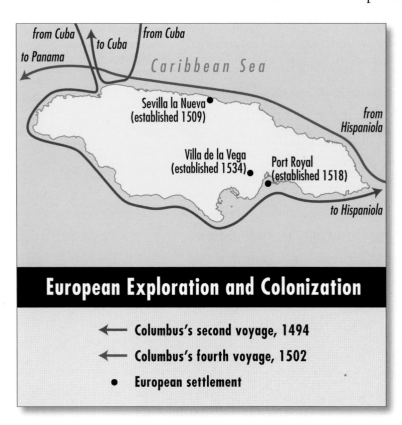

from Cuba
to Panama
to Cuba
from Cuba

Caribbean Sea

Sevilla la Nueva
(established 1509)

from Hispaniola

Villa de la Vega
(established 1534)

Port Royal
(established 1518)

to Hispaniola

European Exploration and Colonization

← Columbus's second voyage, 1494
← Columbus's fourth voyage, 1502
● European settlement

Battling for Control

Meanwhile, Britain, Spain, France, and Holland were competing for control of the Caribbean. In 1655, a British war fleet with eight thousand troops landed in Kingston and marched to Spanish Town. The settlement was nearly deserted, as was most of the rest of the island. The Spanish colonists had set fire to their plantations and freed their slaves. Most of the Spaniards had fled to Cuba and many of the slaves fled to remote areas in the middle of the island.

The British were now in control of Jamaica, but the occupation did not go smoothly. Many British became sick from tropical diseases, and the Africans and Spaniards who remained on the island frequently raided the British settlements. Barely one-quarter of the British who had settled in Jamaica in 1656 were alive a year later.

Port Royal, on the southern coast, was founded in 1518. It was the center of Jamaican shipping throughout the 1600s.

Ruling the Seas

Sea captains in the Caribbean were always on alert for pirates and buccaneers. Pirates were thieves and murderers who raided ships loaded with riches bound for Europe. In the seventeenth century, it was legal for anyone to shoot a pirate on sight. But buccaneers carried letters from foreign governments, giving them a legal right to carry out attacks.

Jamaica's most legendary buccaneer was Henry Morgan (right). Born in Wales, part of Great Britain, Morgan left home to be a pirate and found his way to the Caribbean. He fell into the company of buccaneers such as Calico Jack Rackham, Anne Bonny, Sir Francis Drake, and Bluebeard. With his British license, Henry Morgan led numerous successful attacks on Spanish settlements in Cuba and Panama. In 1674, Henry Morgan was knighted by King Charles II of England. Giving up his career as a buccaneer, Sir Henry Morgan served as Jamaica's deputy governor until his death in 1688.

In 1670, a peace treaty signed by Britain and Spain awarded Jamaica to the British. The British set up several new villages and established Spanish Town as their capital. Despite the treaty, Europeans in the Caribbean continued to clash.

In the midst of these battles, new problems emerged. Gangs of military deserters, convicts, and others turned to piracy. They established secret hideaways on the islands of Tortuga and Hispaniola and survived in the wilderness by hunting wild pigs. They roasted the pigs on a grill called a *boucan*, so in the region they became known as buccaneers. The buccaneers stole ships and weapons throughout the Caribbean.

They looted and terrorized coastal towns and ships at sea. They seized the British fort at Port Royal, near Kingston. Port Royal became known as the richest and most wicked harbor in the Caribbean. British officials were terrified of the buccaneers until they came up with a plan for how to cooperate with them. The British granted licenses to the buccaneers, giving them the authority to attack colonies and ships belonging to the Spanish and Dutch.

Buccaneers working for the British attack a Spanish fleet in the Caribbean.

The Growing Sugar Industry

Sugarcane thrives in tropical climates. Planting, tending, harvesting, and processing sugarcane is grueling work. Sugar plantations had first been established in Jamaica in the early sixteenth century, but it was not until late in the seventeenth century that it became Jamaica's most important crop.

At that time, Britain was pressuring its colonies to increase exports of their goods and natural resources. The British had become especially fond of colonial imports such as cocoa, coffee, and tea. The wealthy upper class enjoyed these tastes all the more when mixed with sugar. Jamaica became the primary exporter of sugar to Britain. To meet Britain's growing demand, British planters in Jamaica brought in enslaved people from West Africa to work on the sugar plantations. Using free slave labor lowered the cost of sugar, which caused the price to fall in

The End of Port Royal

On June 7, 1692, an earthquake struck Port Royal, near Kingston. Port Royal was a key trading port then. Many residents were wealthy merchants, and the population at the time was greater than that of Boston, Massachusetts. The earthquake displaced water in the sea, producing a tsunami, a series of destructive waves. In just minutes, the earthquake and tsunami killed thousands of people. Port Royal was left completely underwater, its buildings destroyed. A group of people hauled a large ship, the HMS *Swan*, up to dry land. It became a refuge for survivors. The village of Port Royal never returned to its former glory.

Britain. As a result, more people could afford sugar so demand for it exploded. In 1700, Britain imported 11 million pounds (5 million kg) of sugar from Jamaica. By 1770, this number had risen to nearly 120 million pounds (55 million kg).

The Triangular Trade

The sugar obsession in Britain created a cycle of horror for Jamaica. Britain imported wood, fur, metals, and other raw materials from its other colonies, which they turned into pots, tools, clothing, and furniture. British manufacturers put their goods on ships bound for West Africa. British shipping merchants sold the goods to slave traders in Africa. After the merchandise was unloaded, enslaved Africans were forced onto the British ships and taken on the second leg of the trade route, to Jamaica. The ships landed in Kingston where the Africans were sold and sugar was loaded onto the ships bound for Britain to complete the third leg of the trip.

The journey across the Atlantic, known as the Middle Passage, was unspeakable in its cruelty. The Africans were chained together and packed tightly onto shelves in the ship's hold. They were underfed and forced to live in darkness and filth for the six- to twelve-week voyage. Many

Triangular Trade

died from starvation, illness, or abuse. Upon arrival in Kingston, the slave traders cleaned the Africans and oiled their skin to make them appear healthy. They auctioned them to buyers from throughout the region. Family members were forced apart, sold to different owners. Slave owners wanted the Africans to feel alone and isolated. This helped the slave owners maintain control.

Slavery and Rebellion

During the eighteenth century, Jamaica was the largest producer of sugar in the world. Plantation owners built grand mansions and usually left the operation of the plantations to overseers. Most overseers were merciless. They forced the enslaved workers to toil from dawn to dark in the blazing heat. Whippings, mutilations, hangings, and other violent punishments were common. Many people were worked to death. After arriving in Jamaica, the average life span of an enslaved African was only seven years.

Conditions were so bad that many Africans chose to risk death in order to escape from the slave owners. One of the first slave uprisings took place in 1690, in Clarendon, on the southern part of the island. Many enslaved people escaped, joining other people who had earlier escaped Spanish slavery, fleeing to the remote interior of the island. They were called the Maroons, from the Spanish word *cimarron*, meaning "wild." The Maroons who lived in the Blue Mountains were called the Windward Maroons and those living in the Cockpit Country were called the Leeward Maroons.

The Maroons were a powerful force against colonial slavery. With their thorough knowledge of the countryside, the Maroons slipped into plantations quietly and attacked by surprise. They burned houses and fields, stole animals, and freed enslaved people. The leader of the Leeward Maroons was a man named Cudjoe. Under his leadership, the Maroons fought the British from 1690 to 1739 in what is known as the First Maroon War. The war ended when the British and Cudjoe signed a peace treaty. Cudjoe agreed to stop the attacks and said he would no longer take in new escapees. Moreover, he promised to help capture escaped slaves. In return, the British gave the Leeward Maroons their freedom and their own land as well as the right to hunt wild pigs and have their own government.

The years following the First Maroon War were less violent, but slavery persisted as the means to wealth for planters, merchants, traders, and sea captains. In 1760, a slave rebellion erupted in Port Maria, on the northern coast. The rebellion was

Maroons in Cockpit Country prepare to attack British forces. Battles flared on and off throughout the eighteenth century as Maroons fought to maintain their independence.

Warrior Queen

The leader of the Windward Maroons was Queen Nanny, a sister of Cudjoe. Nanny was a spiritual leader who practiced Obeah, a West African religion. When Nanny escaped slavery she fled to a remote corner of the Blue Mountains, where she and another brother founded a village they named Nanny Town. She and her followers farmed and traded, living in isolation and peace. But during the First Maroon War, Nanny led attacks on settlements and plantations in order to free slaves. It is believed she was personally responsible for helping nearly 1,000 people escape to safety. According to some sources, the British killed Queen Nanny in 1733, while others say she lived another two decades.

led by an enslaved man named Tacky, who served as the overseer of a plantation. In this position, Tacky was able to communicate secretly with enslaved people on other plantations. Early one morning, Tacky and his followers raided several plantations and freed numerous slaves. But they were soon surrounded. Most of the escaping slaves surrendered and returned to their plantations. But Tacky and several of his men continued to resist and hid near what is now called Tacky Falls. Tacky was killed, but his careful planning inspired many more slave uprisings.

The year 1795 brought about the Second Maroon War, which began when a Maroon was flogged in public for hunting a pig too near a plantation. In response, the Maroons threatened to burn down Montego Bay. The British invaded Maroon settlements in the Cockpit Country. Fighting continued around the island for five months before the Maroons were forced to surrender. The British banished the Maroons and took over their village.

The End of Slavery

In Britain, a group called the Anti-Slavery Society joined with religious groups such as Quakers and Methodists and called for abolition, or a ban on slavery. In 1808, abolitionists convinced their government to end the slave trade. Britain passed laws requiring better treatment of slaves. But many slave owners in Jamaica feared for their livelihood and ignored the laws. Many enslaved people in Jamaica, however, believed that freedom was on its way.

Enslaved Africans harvest sugar in Jamaica. In the early 1800s, enslaved Africans outnumbered whites in Jamaica by more than twenty to one.

Tensions increased, and in 1831 Jamaica's last and largest slave revolt began. The leader of the revolt was Samuel Sharpe, an enslaved worker and Baptist minister in Montego Bay. It was December and he urged his congregation to refuse to work during Christmas week. As word of the resistance spread, British warships filled the harbor. A large estate was burned and bloody fighting raged through the city. In the end, hundreds of people involved in the revolt were executed, including Sharpe, who proclaimed that he "would rather die on yonder gallows than live as a slave." The white response to what is called the Christmas Rebellion so outraged people in Britain that a law was passed officially abolishing slavery in Jamaica in 1834. However, as a concession to the planters, the act said that the former slaves had to work without pay for four more years. In 1838, Africans in Jamaica were finally free.

After 1838, Jamaican planters watched their fortunes crumble. Without free slave labor, the cost of sugar rose and demand fell. The planters signed contracts with indentured servants from Germany, Scotland, Ireland, India, China, and the Middle East. The workers were required to work for seven years before being able to own land and work and live elsewhere. After their contract ended, many chose to leave.

Continuing Trouble

When slavery ended in Jamaica, the island was home to more than 350,000 black people, about 15,000 white people, and 40,000 people of mixed black and white descent, sometimes called mulattoes. Despite their small numbers, Jamaica's white

residents continued to run the government. Blacks were not allowed to vote or hold office. Mulattoes had been given the right to vote in 1830 and tended to support the island's white leadership. Laws were passed denying blacks the right to own land. Unemployment was high and the cost of food was rising.

In 1865, a public protest turned into a bloody riot called the Morant Bay Rebellion. A black minister named Paul Bogle was a spokesman for the rights of black Jamaicans. One of his followers was on trial, and some people had gathered to demonstrate outside the courthouse. Tempers flared between

Angry demonstrators gather outside a courthouse during the Morant Bay Rebellion.

demonstrators and police and a riot broke out. A police station was attacked, and several people were killed. When it was over, the police blamed Paul Bogle, who was hanged. In addition, more than four hundred black Jamaicans were executed, six hundred were publically whipped, and one thousand homes owned by blacks were burnt down. This violent punishment caused an outcry in Britain, and the British government ordered Jamaican lawmakers back to Britain. Britain then established Jamaica as a crown colony, granting Jamaicans many of the same rights as British citizens.

The Crown Colony

Britain appointed Sir John Peter Grant to govern Jamaica. Grant made all the decisions, aided by members of a legislature, whom he chose himself. His government was far from a democracy, but he improved the standard of living in Jamaica. His government created a health system and a fairer judicial system. It built new schools, roads, bridges, and a railroad. Grant and later British leaders helped Jamaica overcome many of the problems that followed abolition. They gave land to the descendants of former slaves and trained them in farm management.

By this time, sugar was no longer the major export from Jamaica. In 1866, an American sea captain loaded his ship with Jamaican bananas and sold them in Boston, Massachusetts. He made such a hefty profit that many farmers changed their crop to bananas. By 1927, Jamaica was exporting more than twenty-one million bunches of bananas every year. In the early twentieth century, fortunes also grew as a growing number of American tourists visited the lush tropical island.

In the early 1900s, an earthquake and fire devastated the capital of Kingston. Then, three years in a row, hurricanes hit the island. In 1929, the American stock market crashed, and Americans could no longer afford sugar, tropical fruits, and vacations. These setbacks put the brakes on Jamaica's budding economy, and unemployment soared. The colonial government, still controlled by the white minority, was unable to solve the island's problems.

An activist named Marcus Garvey encouraged black Jamaicans to speak up for their rights. In 1929, he formed Jamaica's first political party, the People's Political Party. The party called upon the government to allow blacks to vote. Party members also urged Jamaicans to support independence from Britain.

International Hero

Marcus Garvey emerged from the city of St. Ann's Bay to become one of the first major black nationalist leaders. Born in 1887, he grew up in a house full of books. As a teenager, he traveled through Central America and witnessed the poor working and living conditions of black people. He returned to Jamaica and helped establish the Universal Negro Improvement Association in 1914. He said blacks should be proud of their African heritage and that black people needed to start their own businesses and create a separate black economy. In 1916, he took his message to the United States. He was an inspirational speaker, and

many black Americans were encouraged by his ideas of racial equality, unity, and self-reliance. He proposed that descendants of slaves return to Africa and "establish a country and absolute government of their own." By 1920, four million people had joined the Universal Negro Improvement Association.

In 1923, Garvey was convicted of fraud charges related to one of his businesses, and in 1927 the United States sent him back to Jamaica. Back home, he founded the People's Political Party and was elected to local office. Marcus Garvey died in 1940, but his message about being proud of African history, heritage, and culture lived on, inspiring civil rights movements around the world. Marcus Garvey was the first person honored as a national hero by the Jamaican government.

Through protests and strikes, black Jamaicans expressed anger over government inaction and the lack of jobs. In 1938, a major demonstration by job seekers outside a Jamaican sugar factory turned into a deadly riot. Protests spread around the country. A labor leader named Alexander Bustamante became the spokesman for the workers. That same year he founded the first trade union in Jamaica, the Bustamante Industrial Trade Union.

Independence

In 1944, Britain delivered to Jamaica a new constitution giving all adults the right to vote. Over the course of the 1950s, Jamaica gradually gained more independence. In 1958, it became part of the West Indies Federation, a group of Caribbean islands that intended to become independent from Britain. This federation was short-lived, however.

In 1961, Jamaicans voted in favor of leaving the federation, and the following year Jamaica became an independent nation. Bustamante became the nation's first prime minister.

Shifting Power

There were two major political parties in Jamaica: the Jamaica Labor Party (JLP), founded by Bustamante; and the People's National Party (PNP), which had been founded by a lawyer named Norman Manley, who was Bustamante's cousin. In the decades since Jamaica became independent, power has frequently shifted back and forth between the two parties.

Jamaica's economy expanded in the 1960s while the JLP was in power, but unemployment remained high. In 1972,

Children gather around Norman Manley as he heads to the celebration of Jamaican independence in 1962.

Cuban leader Fidel Castro (right) meets with Prime Minister Michael Manley during a visit to Jamaica in 1977. Manley's close relationship with Castro angered U.S. officials, who opposed Castro's communist government.

the PNP won the national elections, and Norman Manley's son Michael became prime minister. The PNP increased the minimum wage and welfare benefits. It promoted literacy campaigns and built public housing. To pay for these programs, the government took over several private companies. Companies that were not taken over were taxed heavily. As a result of such policies, many wealthy and educated people left Jamaica. Manley also established a close relationship with communist leader Fidel Castro of Cuba.

In the middle of the twentieth century, many poor people from rural areas moved to cities looking for work. They found help in the trade unions, each of which was linked to either the JLP or the PNP. The unions built neighborhoods and supplied people with jobs and low-cost housing. Neighborhoods, although very poor, were guarded and gated, making it difficult for outsiders to enter. People started to call the neighborhoods "garrisons."

By 1976, the rivalry between the two parties and their supporters had grown so violent that Manley declared a state of emergency and sent soldiers and police into the streets to protect voters on election day. Political conflict grew worse, especially in Kingston and Spanish Town. Garrison leaders encouraged their supporters to recruit voters and to drive away opposition. Before long, garrisons became dangerously powerful. Guns and threats led to crime and gangs. During the 1980 elections, hundreds of people were shot in gang killings.

A policeman (right) watches over a voting place during the 1976 elections in Jamaica.

The JLP, then led by Edward Seaga, won the 1980 elections. Seaga wanted to improve relations with the United States, so he pulled away from Cuba. Because of Seaga's opposition to communism, the United States provided Jamaica with aid. The government cut spending in the 1980s, and some of these changes angered citizens. In 1989, Jamaicans voted the PNP back into power.

In the 1990s, the economy slumped. Many poor people lost their jobs, and some believed that the trade unions and political parties were not helping. They looked instead to the gangs in their garrisons for aid. Gang leaders made money through drugs and crime, but they spread the money around the community, providing jobs and funding health clinics and community centers.

Recent Times

The poverty of the garrisons and crime in the cities remain huge challenges for Jamaica. The nation is also trying to spur economic growth. Jamaica faltered during a worldwide economic downturn that lasted from about 2007 to 2009.

In recent years, the nation's tourism and farming sectors have been growing. Roads have been upgraded, hotels have been built, and in 2011, a port opened in Falmouth, on the northern coast, that can handle the largest of cruise ships. Many Jamaicans are seeing their livelihoods improve. Since independence, Jamaicans have not been content to let problems go unsolved, just as during their turbulent history, they were not afraid to rise up and speak out.

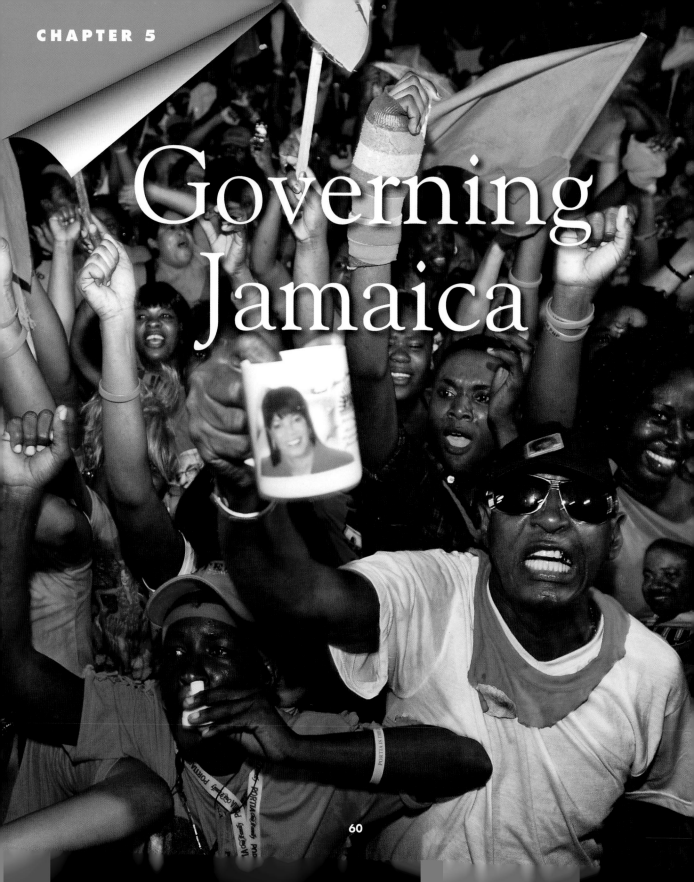

CHAPTER 5

Governing Jamaica

JAMAICA DID NOT FIGHT A WAR TO WIN INDEPENDENCE, but it suffered under centuries of harsh colonial rule before becoming an independent nation. Jamaicans gained the right to govern themselves on August 6, 1962. Although independent, Jamaica belongs to the Commonwealth, a group of nations once ruled by Great Britain. Commonwealth nations maintain a close relationship with Great Britain and consider the British monarch their head of state.

The constitution of Jamaica grants basic rights to its citizens, such as life, liberty, freedom of speech, the right of peaceful assembly, and freedom of movement. The constitution forbids inhumane treatment and racial, gender, and political discrimination.

Opposite: **Supporters of the People's National Party cheer following their election victory in 2011. The PNP has been the leading party in Jamaica for all but four years since 1989.**

The Jamaican flag bears a diagonal cross, dividing it into four sections. The upper and lower sections are green, the left and right sections are black, and the cross is gold. It is generally believed that the gold symbolizes sunlight, the green symbolizes the island's lush vegetation and abundant farmlands, and the black represents the hardships faced by its people.

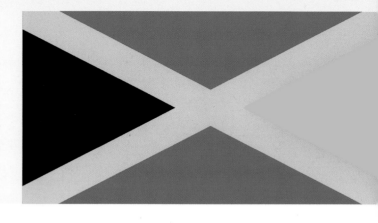

The Monarchy

The Jamaican constitution outlines the role of the monarch and appointees within the government. The British monarch, currently Queen Elizabeth II, is the symbolic head of state. The monarch appoints a governor-general to act as head of state. The governor-general, with advice from the prime minister,

Queen Elizabeth II speaks with Patrick Allen, who became governor-general of Jamaica in 2009.

National Government of Jamaica

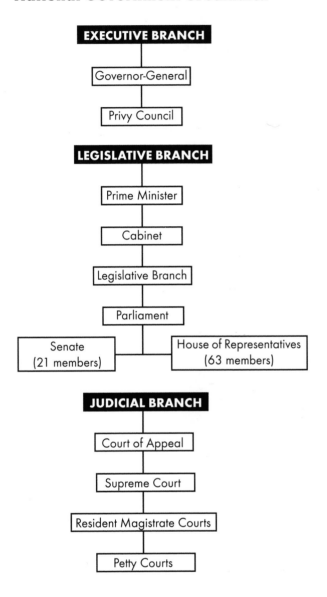

EXECUTIVE BRANCH

Governor-General

Privy Council

LEGISLATIVE BRANCH

Prime Minister

Cabinet

Legislative Branch

Parliament

Senate
(21 members)

House of Representatives
(63 members)

JUDICIAL BRANCH

Court of Appeal

Supreme Court

Resident Magistrate Courts

Petty Courts

appoints a six-member Privy Council to advise him or her. The governor-general cannot be a member of any political party. Neither the monarch nor the governor-general can take an active role in ruling the country. The position of governor-

general is ceremonial. Formal duties include officially signing bills into law, attending state dinners and parades, awarding medals and honors, opening sessions of parliament with a speech called the Throne Speech, and dissolving parliament.

The Legislative Branch

The legislative, or lawmaking, branch of the Jamaican government is called a parliament. The Jamaican Parliament is made up of two houses, the Senate and the House of Representatives. The party with the most votes controls the parliament. The parties with fewer votes unite to form the opposition party.

Queen Elizabeth II addressed the Jamaican Parliament during a visit in 2002.

The Senate has twenty-one members. Senators are appointed, not elected. Although the governor-general formally makes the appointments, the leaders of the political parties guide the selection process. There are thirteen senators from the majority party and eight from the opposition party. The Senate's role is usually to review bills proposed by the House of Representatives. Senators may propose their own bills. However, because the senators have not been elected by the people, they cannot propose a budget or tax bill.

The sixty-three members of the House of Representatives are elected. Each house member represents a certain region, called a constituency. The members of the House select a leader called the Speaker of the House. The Speaker makes certain that rules of order are being followed. The Speaker does not generally participate in discussions.

A parliament can last a maximum of five years. After that, it must be dissolved and new elections held. If a majority of members of the House of Representatives have lost confidence in the government, the parliament can be dissolved early and new elections called.

A voter casts his ballot in elections for the House of Representatives.

Portia Simpson Miller has twice served as prime minister of Jamaica. She believes Jamaica should end its relationship with the British monarchy and instead have an elected head of state.

The Executive Branch

The prime minister, the leader of the majority party in parliament, is the acting head of government. Besides advising the governor-general on appointees, the prime minister appoints members of the cabinet. The cabinet consists of eleven to fifteen ministers who oversee different parts of government such as foreign affairs, national security, health, agriculture, tourism, and education. The prime minister is also the chief spokesperson of the government at home and abroad. In 2006, Portia Simpson Miller of the PNP became the first female prime minister of Jamaica. She began a second term in 2012.

The Judicial Branch

The judicial system in Jamaica is divided into several different levels. The highest court in Jamaica is the Court of Appeal,

National Anthem

The national anthem of Jamaica is "Jamaica, Land We Love." The words are by Hugh Braham Sherlock, and the music is by Robert Charles Lightbourne. It was adopted in 1962.

Eternal Father bless our land,
Guard us with Thy mighty hand,
Keep us free from evil powers,
Be our light through countless hours.
To our leaders, Great Defender,
Grant true wisdom from above.

Justice, truth be ours forever,
Jamaica, land we love.
Jamaica, Jamaica, Jamaica, land we love.

Teach us true respect for all,
Stir response to duty's call,
Strengthen us the weak to cherish,
Give us vision lest we perish.
Knowledge send us, Heavenly Father,
Grant true wisdom from above.

Justice, truth be ours forever,
Jamaica, land we love.
Jamaica, Jamaica, Jamaica, land we love.

A Look at the Capital

Kingston, the capital of Jamaica, is also its largest city, with a population of 666,041 in 2011. It is the largest English-speaking city in the Western Hemisphere south of the United States.

Kingston was founded in 1692 after nearby Port Royal was destroyed by an earthquake. It has served as the capital of Jamaica since 1872. Many of the city's historic buildings were destroyed in an earthquake in 1907.

The city lies on Jamaica's southern coast, on an excellent natural harbor. It is the nation's major port as well as its economic and cultural center. Major tourist sites in Kingston include the Museums of History and Ethnography; Hope Gardens, one of the largest botanical gardens in the Caribbean; and the Bob Marley Museum, which is located in a house where Marley, Jamaica's most famous musician, once lived.

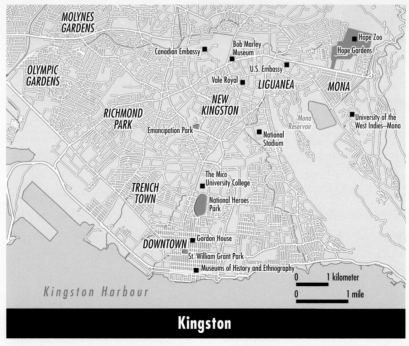

Kingston

which reviews and corrects decisions made in lower courts. In rare cases, judgments made in the Court of Appeal can themselves be appealed to the Privy Council.

The Supreme Court is the highest trial court in the land. It handles both civil and criminal cases, as well as cases related to tax law, family law, and other issues. Less serious cases are heard in one of the fourteen resident magistrate courts. After receiving a judgment in a magistrate court, citizens may appeal directly to the Court of Appeal. The lowest court in Jamaica is called petty court. Justices of the peace in petty courts rule on cases such as disorderly conduct and disturbing the peace. Citizens may not appeal a petty court ruling.

Local Government

When the British colonized Jamaica, each church on the island served a particular community, called a parish. The British used the parish borders to create administrative borders. The number of parishes changed through the years. Today, the island is still divided into fourteen parishes, although now they mark only government divisions and not religious ones. Each parish has its own capital, local government council, and magistrate court.

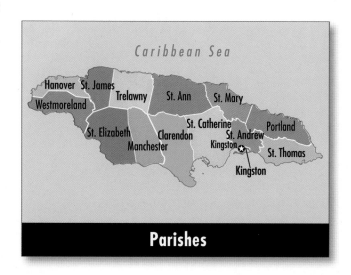

Caribbean Sea

Hanover St. James
Westmoreland
Trelawny
St. Ann
St. Mary
St. Elizabeth
St. Catherine
Clarendon
Manchester
St. Andrew
Kingston
Portland
Kingston
St. Thomas

Parishes

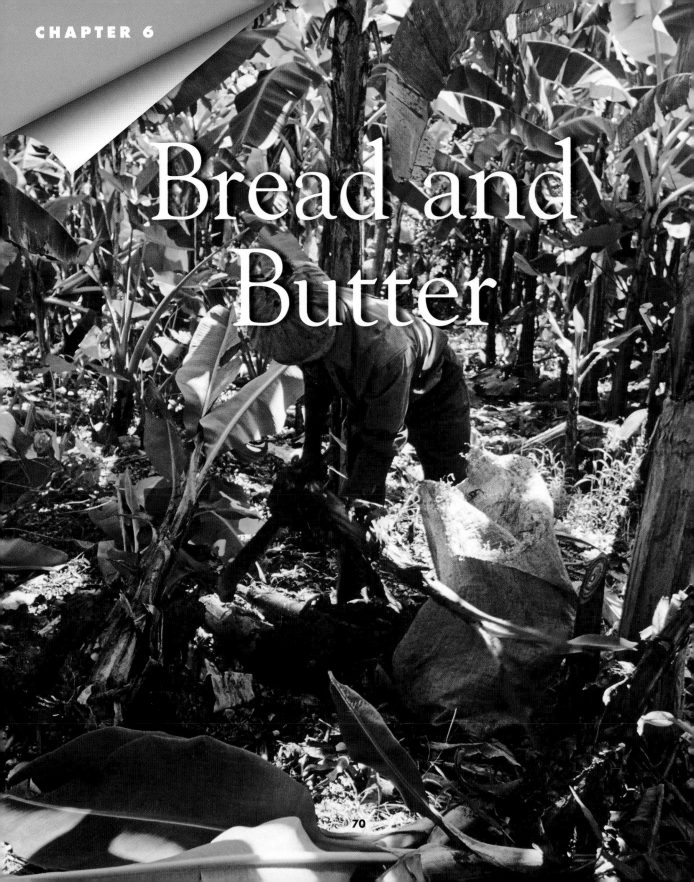

CHAPTER 6

Bread and Butter

JAMAICA IS A BEAUTIFUL ISLAND WITH TURQUOISE water, white sand beaches, graceful mansions, and luxury resorts. But it is also a country with a struggling economy and high unemployment. Although they face some serious difficulties, Jamaicans are creative and hardworking, and show great determination to make their country grow and prosper.

Opposite: **A farmer prunes banana leaves, which often grow 9 feet (2.7 m) long.**

From the Land

Agriculture is a small but vital part of Jamaica's economy. Jamaican farmers grow sugarcane, bananas, yams, coconuts, citrus fruits, vegetables, spices, coffee, and cacao, which is used to make chocolate. The country is also home to many dairy, cattle, chicken, fish, and shellfish farms.

Many Jamaican products are sold for export, including sugarcane, bananas, spices, and coffee. Blue Mountain coffee is particularly valuable. In 1728, the king of France gave the governor of Jamaica a prized coffee plant. The governor planted it on his estate near the Blue Mountains and the coffee thrived in the cool, wet climate, rich volcanic soil, and high altitudes. Blue Mountain coffee beans command a high price and are considered among the finest in the world.

Though Jamaica is a land with rich soil and abundant sunshine and fresh water, the United States supplies nearly one-half of all the nation's food. Many Jamaicans, including people in the government, are urging citizens to look toward self-sustaining food production.

Most Jamaican farmers work small plots of land. They grow enough to feed their families and to sell at local markets, but they do not grow enough to feed all the people.

Workers harvest coffee beans in the Blue Mountains. After the red beans are picked, they are soaked to remove the fleshy outside. The seed inside is used to make coffee.

The government has been developing programs to help small farmers. No one wants to see the rural way of life disappear. It is hoped that the two hundred thousand small farmers in the country will band together and form farmers' cooperatives, where they can pool their money and buy fertilizer at lower prices and share the cost of high-tech farm machinery. By increasing their production, farmers' incomes will grow. Similarly, other Jamaicans may be able to save money because they will not have to buy expensive imported food.

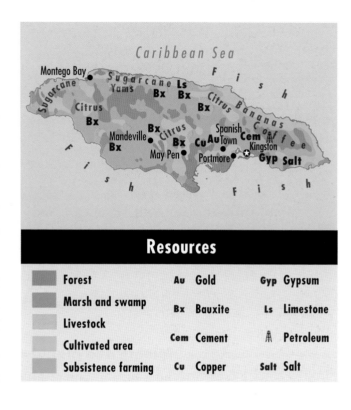

Resources

Forest	Au	Gold	Gyp	Gypsum
Marsh and swamp	Bx	Bauxite	Ls	Limestone
Livestock				
Cultivated area	Cem	Cement	🛢	Petroleum
Subsistence farming	Cu	Copper	Salt	Salt

Grow What We Eat

Nearly five hundred schools in Jamaica grow their own food in gardens on school grounds, and that number is increasing year by year. Students tend crops and raise poultry, and are rewarded with eggs, fruits, and vegetables that are served in their cafeterias (called "canteens" in Jamaica). Some student farmers produce more than their school needs so they sell the excess at local markets, making money for school programs. "Grow what we eat and eat what we grow" is the program's motto.

A power shovel pours bauxite into a dump truck in Jamaica. Bauxite is usually found near the surface of the earth.

Mining and Manufacturing

In 1942, a Jamaican farmer and businessperson had his soil tested to see how he could improve his crop production. The test results showed that his rich, red soil contained many minerals including bauxite, an ore that contains alumina, which is used to make aluminum. Aluminum at that time was in high demand for use in military manufacturing of warplanes and weapons. The mineral became the property of the British government. The British never mined Jamaica's bauxite, but in the 1950s, several American aluminum producers began mining and importing the ore. Jamaica is now one of the world's leading producers of bauxite, mining more than 10 million metric tons each year.

Alumina is removed from bauxite in a process that leaves behind large quantities of red mud mining waste called tailings. In 2012, researchers discovered that the red mud contained rare earth elements, which are metals that are used in the manufacture of smartphones, computers, televisions, cars, satellites, and much more. Work is now underway to determine how to extract the rare earth elements from the red mud and turn it into a profitable new industry.

Jamaica also mines limestone, which is used in agriculture, glassmaking, and building construction; gypsum, which is used to make cement and other building materials; and marble, which is used in luxury building construction. On a smaller scale, Jamaica mines silica, copper, iron, lead, and zinc. All together, mining is the second-largest industry in the country, after tourism.

What Jamaica Grows, Makes, and Mines

AGRICULTURE (2011)

Sugarcane	1,518,300 metric tons
Coconuts	290,000 metric tons
Yams	134,620 metric tons

MANUFACTURING (2008)

Cement	724,600,000 metric tons
Sugar	140,000 metric tons
Flour	132,561 metric tons

MINING (2011)

Bauxite	10,190,000 metric tons
Limestone	2,200,000 metric tons
Gypsum	96,000 metric tons

Workers prepare scotch bonnet peppers, a vital ingredient in Jamaican cuisine. Food processing is a major industry in Jamaica.

Manufacturing accounts for about 8 percent of the Jamaican economy. Major products include processed foods such as sugar, molasses, and rum. Chemicals, construction materials, plastic goods, and textiles are also produced in Jamaica.

Money Facts

The Jamaican unit of currency is the Jamaican dollar, which is often abbreviated J$. Each dollar is divided into 100 cents. Coins come in values of 1, 10, and 25 cents, which are rarely used, and 1, 5, 10, and 20 dollars. Bills come in values of 50, 100, 500, 1,000, and 5,000 dollars. Each bill shows an image of a prominent Jamaican on the front and depicts a site of natural or historic importance on the back. The J$50 bill, for example, shows Samuel Sharpe, the leader of the Christmas Rebellion, on the front and Doctors Cave Beach on the back. All of the bills also show the Jamaican coat of arms. The coat of arms includes a Taino man and woman, a pineapple (representing abundant vegetation), a crocodile (representing native animals), and a helmet and cloak (in recognition of Great Britain). In 2014, J$113 equaled US$1.

Tourism and Other Services

Nearly half of all Jamaicans are either directly or indirectly employed in the tourism industry. Tourism is one of Jamaica's major service industries. These are industries in which people do things for other people rather than growing or building products. Banking, education, and health care are also important service industries in Jamaica.

A doctor examines a patient in Montego Bay.

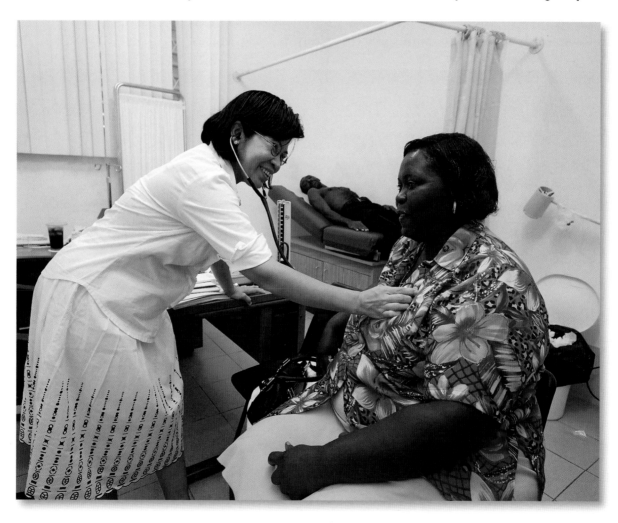

In the tourist sector, people work at hotels, resorts, tourist attractions, and tour guide companies, and on cruise ships. Many other workers earn a living from tourism by being farmers, restaurant workers, transportation workers, craftspeople, and shipping, port, and airport workers.

Each year more than two million tourists visit Jamaica. They come to the small villages and large cities, guesthouses, hotels, campgrounds, and luxury resorts. In Jamaica, tourists swim, golf, play tennis, ride horses, fish, dive, and hike. A

Tourists relax on the beautiful beaches of Montego Bay, on Jamaica's northern coast. Montego Bay welcomes more tourists than any other part of Jamaica.

growing form of Jamaican tourism is ecotourism. Environmentalists say that big resorts put a burden on the environment with roadways, water pollution, and sprawling developments that destroy wild habitats. Many ecotourists try to experience nature without damaging the environment. They might hike, bike, bird-watch, kayak, sail, or raft. Ecotourist lodgings are careful to conserve resources such as water, electricity, and fuel.

Communications

Jamaica has three major newspapers, the *Jamaica Gleaner*, the *Jamaica Observer*, and the *Jamaica Star*. There are several TV stations and dozens of radio stations.

A man reads a newspaper in Kingston.

Almost everyone in Jamaica has a cell phone. This allows them to easily keep in touch with relatives who move away. Social media also plays an important role in bringing Jamaicans together. In 2013, Tessanne Chin won *The Voice*, the TV singing competition, in part by using social media to encourage Jamaicans to watch the show and vote for her. Many other Jamaican celebrities, including runner Usain Bolt and musician Sean Paul, are avid Instagram users.

CHAPTER 7

One People

"OUT OF MANY, ONE PEOPLE," THE NATIONAL motto of Jamaica, reflects the country's diverse heritage. Jamaica was created by people from a host of different ethnic groups: Tainos; Spanish and British colonists; enslaved West Africans; Asian and European indentured servants; European Jews; and Lebanese, Syrian, and Palestinian refugees. Jamaica's many ethnic groups brought their own traditions, languages, and values, and, in time, the parts became a whole. In 2014, Jamaica had an estimated population of 2,930,050.

Opposite: **Schoolchildren at St. Ann's Bay in northern Jamaica**

Ethnicity in Jamaica (2011)*	
Black	92.1%
East Indian	0.8%
Mixed	6.1%
Chinese	0.2%
White	0.2%
Other	0.1%
No answer	0.7%

*Total does not equal 100% because of rounding.

Tainos

The Taino people laid the foundation for what is now Jamaica. Although most Tainos did not survive the Spanish invasion of the island, some retreated into hiding and were later joined by Maroons. The Tainos taught the Maroons how to survive in the wilderness and shared their knowledge of medicinal plants

Spanish Town features many historic buildings, including the cathedral.

and spiritual rituals. Many English words, including canoe, hurricane, tobacco, barbecue, and hammock, have their roots in the Taino language.

Europeans

In Jamaica, the Spanish colonizers focused on farming in order to send supplies to their other colonies. The Spanish introduced fruit trees, cattle, and sugar to the island. The Spanish presence is also visible in some of the ornate buildings in Spanish Town, the former capital, including the governor's house and the cathedral. Many buildings throughout the island show a Spanish influence, especially in the use of tile roofs and decorative iron gates.

The three hundred years of British colonization have had an enormous impact on Jamaica. The country's official language is English. Jamaica's government, judicial system, military, and police are modeled after the British systems. Schools and most churches are British in nature. Nearly all place-names in Jamaica date to the period of British rule.

Many Europeans arrived as indentured servants, and later added their touch to the Jamaican way of life. For example, Irish priests and nuns taught in Catholic schools throughout the island for generations, and, as a result, most Jamaicans speak with the lilt of an Irish accent.

European Jews escaped persecution in Europe in the six-teenth century and sought freedom to practice their religion

Jamaican soldiers prepare for inspection. The Jamaican military has traditions similiar to those of the British military, and soldiers studying to be officers often train in England.

in Jamaica. Over the centuries, they became established members of the community. By 1849, eight of the forty-seven members of the colonial assembly were Jewish. These members were so highly regarded that the assembly closed in honor of the Jewish holy day Yom Kippur.

Asians

After slavery ended in Jamaica, white planters brought Chinese and East Indian indentured servants to work on their plantations. Many remained in Jamaica after their servitude ended. The Chinese influenced Jamaicans with their values

A Jamaican man of Chinese descent. Chinese people first immigrated to Jamaica in the mid-1800s.

Connections to the Past

Although many Jamaican towns bear British names, others have different connections.

Town	Origin
Madras, Bengal	India (names of cities)
Aberdeen	Scotland (city)
Llandovery	Wales (town)
Ballyholly	Ireland (town)
Catherine's Peak	Catherine Long, wife of buccaneer Henry Morgan, was the first woman to scale this peak
Ocho Rios	Spain (meaning "eight rivers")
Guanaboa	Taino (meaning "house of gold")
Accompong	Africa (meaning "lone warrior")

Black Jamaicans, like their African forebears, sometimes gave towns descriptive names: Rest-and-Be-Thankful, Broke Neck Gully, Excellent Town, Rat Trap, Shambles, Putogether Corner, and Me-No-Sen-You-No-Come (a Maroon town whose name means "keep out").

such as the importance of hard work, the extended family, and education. East Indians made contributions to Jamaican society as artisans, merchants, manufacturers, scientists, and farmers. They introduced rice and other foods now central to Jamaican cooking.

Lebanese, Syrians, and Palestinians migrated to Jamaica from southwestern Asia in the nineteenth century to escape religious persecution. They brought traditional foods that became a part of Jamaican cuisine. Many Lebanese, Syrians, and Palestinians became successful manufacturers, merchants, and business owners. Edward Seaga, the longest-serving member of the parliament and a former prime minister, is of Lebanese heritage.

Jamaican culture has a strong connection to Africa.

Africans

People of African descent are the dominant ethnic group in Jamaica today. They are descended from West African ethnic groups such as the Igbo and Yoruba of Nigeria and the Akan of Ghana. While the British established the formal structure of Jamaican society, black Jamaicans created the feel of the culture, through religion, art, music, food, styles of dress, social relationships, family structure, and language.

This Jamaican culture developed over time. When enslaved Africans first arrived, they were separated from their families and other members of their ethnic group and taken to plantations to live among strangers. The enslaved people had no choice but to adapt to one another and create a new society. They created new traditions for courtship, marriage, childrearing, and burying the dead. They shared their knowledge of healing and taught others the music, dance, stories, and prayers from their own ethnic group. They also had to learn to communicate with one another, and with the plantation owners. A new language was born, now known as either Jamaican, Jamaican patois, or Jamaican Creole.

Jamaican Language

The Jamaican language developed out of the need for the planters and the enslaved Africans to communicate with each other. They took words from each other's languages, exchanged grammar rules, accents, and pronunciations, added facial and hand movements, and used phonetic spelling. Most people describe this language as a patois, or dialect, invented for communication between people who do not speak each other's language. However, language experts say that Jamaican is more than a patois. Instead, it is a creole language, a language which developed over time from different influences.

Everyday Jamaican Expressions

Wha' gwan?	What's going on?
Wha' pen?	What's happening?
Ever'ting criss.	Everything looks good.
All fruits ripe.	Everything is good/appealing.
Cool runnings.	Have a safe trip.
Likkle more.	See you later.
Walk good.	Good-bye, be safe.

Jamaican Proverbs

Jamaican is a colorful language. It is rich in tone, rhythm, humor, and wit. Here are some Jamaican expressions and proverbs:

"From mi yeye deh a mi knee."

Translation: From my eyes were at my knees

Meaning: From when I was very young

"Yu tink seh mi born big?"

Translation: You think I was born big (old)?

Meaning: I'm not a fool, I wasn't born yesterday!

"Wan, Wan coco full bahskit."

Translation: One, one coconut, full basket

Meaning: Every little bit counts.

"De ola de moon, de brighter de shine."

Translation: The older the moon, the brighter the shine.

Meaning: The older a person is, the wiser.

"A nuh every'ting soak up waata a sponge."

Translation: Not everything that soaks up water is a sponge.

Meaning: Things are not always what they seem, look carefully before you choose.

"Day langa dan rope."

Translation: The day is longer than rope.

Meaning: Even if it takes a while, wrongs will be made right.

All Jamaicans today speak and understand English. People in government, business, education, and professional jobs tend to speak only English. However, rural people, inner-city dwellers, and young people tend to speak both English and Jamaican Creole.

City and Country

Nearly 50 percent of all Jamaicans live in either Kingston or in one of the fourteen parish capitals. City life offers hope and opportunity—a chance for a better education, a better job, wealth, and success.

Kingston, the capital, is home to about one-fifth of all Jamaicans. The city is divided in half. One-half bustles with commerce, government offices, fine restaurants, theaters, and museums. Wealthier people live high up on the hills overlooking the harbor or in suburban neighborhoods.

Yet mere blocks away are hundreds of thousands of people living in run-down housing. After independence, thousands of rural poor people moved to Kingston in search of work. A few were able to move into new government-built housing complexes. But most lived in tin-roofed shacks, called shanties, that

Population of Major Cities (2011 est.)	
Kingston	666,041
Portmore	182,153
Spanish Town	147,152
Montego Bay	110,115
May Pen	61,548

Some neighborhoods of Kingston are filled with run-down houses.

they built themselves. Neighborhoods of these shacks are called shantytowns. Today, those neighborhoods are overcrowded, poor, and crime-ridden. The rural poor continue to come to Kingston, and the shantytowns continue to expand. The divide between rich and poor in Kingston is striking. Most Kingston residents only know "their" half of the city and never visit the other half.

Though many people from rural areas have moved to the city, the country is never far away. Most people have large extended families in the country, and they visit them often. The country gives city people a chance to relax and enjoy nature.

Some Jamaicans who live in towns and villages live near large resorts and hold service jobs or work at restaurants, markets, and tourist attractions. Unlike the tourists who must soon head home, the local people can enjoy the beautiful weather, beaches, mountains, rivers, and lush vegetation throughout the year. Other Jamaicans who live in villages and towns live a much more rural life. Many fish or own small plots of land that they farm. Their crops feed their families and earn them extra money at the market.

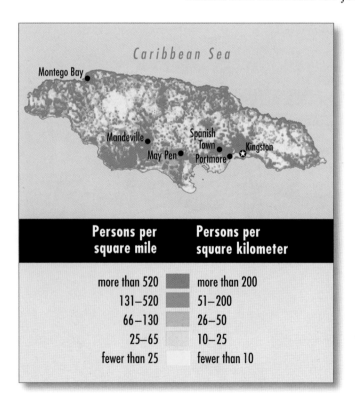

Persons per square mile		Persons per square kilometer
more than 520		more than 200
131–520		51–200
66–130		26–50
25–65		10–25
fewer than 25		fewer than 10

Education

Jamaican children attend primary school from grades one to six. Students take standardized tests

A Jamaican student prepares for an exam.

each year. Test scores are published in the local newspapers, encouraging students to do their best. In sixth grade, students take an entrance exam in order to attend secondary school. Students choose five schools they would like to attend and the schools make their selections based on students' test scores. Once in secondary school, each year in school is called a form. When they reach forms 4 and 5 (grades 10 to 11), students elect many of their courses, including vocational classes. Form 6 is optional and is equivalent to grades 12 to 13. It is very competitive.

Students who want to have a higher education must take a test called the Caribbean Advanced Proficiency Examination (CAPE), which is considered more difficult than most exams taken in universities. Jamaica has seven colleges and universities, several teachers' colleges, and more than a dozen community colleges.

CHAPTER 8

The Spiritual World

On Sundays, in cities and towns throughout Jamaica, people make their way to church, many wearing their best clothes. There are more than 1,600 churches on the island representing a wide variety of religious groups. Although most Jamaicans are Christian, each faith, in its own way, reflects the country's past.

Taino Beliefs

Jamaica has been an intensely spiritual home to inhabitants ever since the first people arrived. The Taino people believed in the divine. They painted their gods' likenesses on walls and in caves. They created idols, called *zemis*, from wood, stone, shells, coral, gold, clay, and bones. Some zemis had human faces, while others were symbols of the natural world, such as mountains and plants. Different zemis had different powers, such as guarding children, crops, and homes or delivering victory at war. Zemis were honored in special buildings and in ceremonies where people made food offerings, sang, danced, and told stories.

Roman Catholics and Jews

The Spanish occupation of Jamaica took place during the time of the Spanish Inquisition in Europe. The Inquisition was a court system controlled by the Catholic Church that was used to punish anyone who was not a believer. The Spanish colonizers, believing in the supremacy of the Catholic Church, attempted to convert the Tainos, but many refused to give up their traditional faith and were murdered. The Spaniards built a grand cathedral in Spanish Town and established small chapels throughout the island.

The Shaare Shalom Synagogue in Kingston is the last active synagogue, or Jewish house of worship, in Jamaica.

Some Spanish and Portuguese Jews escaped the Inquisition and joined the Catholic colonizers in Jamaica. They were called *conversos*, and had to pretend to be Catholics, all the while practicing their faith in secret.

When the British took over Jamaica, the Catholic Church was banned in Britain and all its colonies, forcing Jamaican Catholics to practice their religion in secret. In 1791, Britain reversed its ban. Freedom of religion was now the rule. Catholics could once again practice their religion in Jamaica.

Jews were also able to worship openly, and they built several synagogues. Today, Jamaican Jews are called the United Congregation of Israelites. Their synagogue in Kingston, Shaare Shalom, is renowned for its sand floor. There are two explanations for the sand. The first is that the Jamaican Jews are so far from the desert holy land that they feel the need to walk on sand. The second is that the sand represents the time when Jamaican Jews had to keep their gatherings hidden. Walking on sand would muffle their footsteps, and their prints were easily covered over afterward.

The Africans saw similarities between Catholic rituals and the religious practices they left behind in Africa, such as burning incense, lighting candles, worshipping with music, and chanting. Like the African village holy men, Catholic priests wore flowing robes and called upon spirits. But the Catholic Church in Jamaica was run by a small group of whites who still felt persecuted by the British. They chose to keep their congregations small and did not try to convert blacks or accept other whites into their midst. Between the 1940s and 1950s,

A Jamaican family attends Mass at a Catholic church in Seaford Town, in western Jamaica.

Lebanese and Chinese immigrants converted to Catholicism, yet today, there are still just a few Roman Catholic churches in Jamaica.

Protestants

Protestant Christianity is the most common religion in Jamaica today. More Jamaicans are followers of the Church of God than any other church. But the Anglican Church, also called the Church of England, was once the most widespread. The Church of England was the church of the British colonizers. In the 1700s, British church officials wanted their ministers in the colonies to teach and convert the slaves. The Jamaican planters would have none of it. But Baptist preachers George Liele and Moses Baker brought Christian teachings to enslaved people throughout Jamaica. The people responded to the ideas that all people were equal in God's eyes and that slavery was wrong. The Baptist ministers told the Old Testament Bible story of the enslaved Israelites in Egypt who believed that a savior, a Messiah, would free them. After slavery ended, it was the Baptists, Methodists, and Presbyterians that the newly freed people turned to for spiritual guidance.

In the late 1850s, a Christian movement called the Great Revival spread across the United States and parts of Europe before arriving in Jamaica in 1860. The movement was a stirring call to accept Christianity. Jamaicans filled Protestant churches to hear the promise that their sins would be forgiven and that they would achieve eternal salvation. The prayer meetings were very vocal and lively. To black Jamaicans, this spiritual energy stirred up memories of African worship and rituals. During the revival, Protestant and African belief

Bringing the Word

George Liele was an enslaved American who was also a Baptist minister. Liele was freed during the American Revolution, but after the war, his former owner's family wanted to return him to slavery. A departing British colonel offered to pay his passage to Jamaica if he would work as an indentured servant for two years. Liele and his family agreed, and they set sail with evacuating troops for Kingston.

As promised, Liele was released after two years, and he soon devoted himself to preaching the Bible to the enslaved Jamaicans. With the help of sympathetic British Baptist and Methodist missionaries, Liele built small churches and schools. He baptized thousands of enslaved people and ordained others as ministers.

In 1805, Jamaica passed a law that forbade preaching to slaves. This only encouraged more activism among black preachers and British missionaries, and the campaign to end slavery went into full force.

systems blended and created a new, vibrant, and distinctly Jamaican manner of worship that exists to this day.

Revivalism

There are three Christian Revivalist groups practicing in Jamaica today, called Revival, Zion, and Kumina (sometimes Pocomania or Pukkumina). They share many beliefs and practices, such as a focus on dreams, visions, and miracles.

The Revivalist groups are led by shepherds or shepherdesses, who wear special garments and large turbans. They are

A person is baptized at a Protestant church in Montego Bay. The majority of Jamaicans are Protestant.

preachers, teachers, healers, and judges. A typical service begins with Bible readings and prayers, followed by singing hymns and chanting. While drums, cymbals, tambourines, and other instruments play, worshippers move counterclockwise, dancing in a manner called "tramping and travailing." As they move and sing, their passion grows, and many hope to be possessed by guiding spirits by the time the music stops. People who practice these religions believe that spirits sometimes speak through the dancers, telling the future or forecasting disasters, such as illness, death, earthquakes, or hurricanes. Kumina dancing is particularly intense, and dancers strive to reach a state called *myal*, where it is believed that the spirits of ancestors take hold of the dancer's body. In this case, the dancer appears to lose control of speech and movement and falls into a trance.

Kumina is mainly practiced in urban areas, especially Kingston. Zion and Revival groups have members throughout the island. Four times each year, large gatherings occur in St. Ann Parish, where Revivalism first took hold.

Rastafarians

Rastafarianism, a religion that began in Jamaica, combines Christianity, mysticism, and a strong connection to Africa. The religion emerged in the early twentieth century, when Marcus Garvey was urging black people to honor their African past and return to their ancestral home. In 1930, Ras Tafari Makonnen (*ras* is an Ethiopian title similar to a duke) was crowned Emperor of Ethiopia and took the name Haile

Jamaican Religion (2011 est.)*	
Protestant	64.8%
Roman Catholic	2.2%
Jehovah's Witness	1.9%
Rastafarian	1.1%
Other	6.5%
None	21.3%
Unspecified	2.3%

*Total does not equal 100% because of rounding.

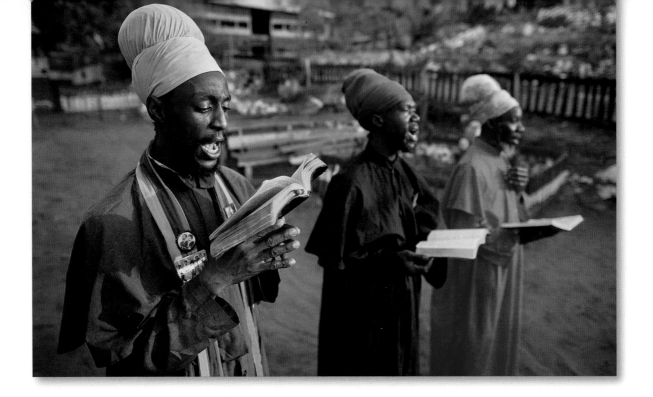

Rastafarians chant readings from the Bible. Rastas accept much of the Bible, but they believe its teachings have been misinterpreted.

Selassie I. The faithful in Jamaica believed that Ethiopia was the ultimate home of all Africans and that Haile Selassie would lead them to the Promised Land, so they called themselves Rastafarians.

Followers of Rastafarianism, called Rastas, believe in one god, whom they call Jah. Although Rastas oppose the dominance white people have in society, they are accepting of others and preach love and nonviolence. They are earnest students of the Bible and are often seen carrying one as they go about their day. Rastas believe that the divine resides in each person and in all living things.

Most Rastas are vegetarians, but those who do eat meat do not eat pork, since pigs are scavengers. Rastas eat fish but not crabs or lobster, because they are scavengers of the sea. Rastas do not drink coffee or alcohol or smoke tobacco.

Rastas like to show their commitment through symbolic gestures. Many wear a Star of David. Their clothing is often red, green, and gold, the colors of the Ethiopian flag. Like the style of dress in the Bible, the men wear beards and have long hair, which they weave into thick braids called dreadlocks, or dreads for short. Many devout Rastas wear large hats, head wraps, or turbans over their bound-up dreads. A Rastafari group called the Bobo Shanti sells handmade brooms as part of its livelihood. Some believe the broom is a symbol of cleanliness. The Rastafarian movement continues to gather new believers. Today, there are more than one million Rastas around the world. Some of the style of Rastafarianism has spread in Jamaica, beyond people who practice the religion. Dreads and red, green, and gold clothing are popular among many young people in Jamaica.

Obeah

Obeah (depicted in the musical *Obeah Opera*, left) is a spiritual belief system derived from some West African religious practices and used in Jamaica and other parts of the Caribbean. Obeah practitioners use herbs, charms, potions, candles, chants, and folk medicine to try to help their followers. Believers say that Obeah practitioners channel the supernatural. Some say they cast spells or use magic. People seek them out to help protect their families, get a job or make money, change their luck, fall in love, or remove a curse or curse an enemy. Some people in Jamaica consider Obeah witchcraft, and it is illegal. But the practice lives on, and there are countless secret Obeah shops around the island.

CHAPTER 9

Rich Life

JAMAICAN CULTURE IS A VIBRANT EXPRESSION OF A vibrant people. The island inspires writers, artists, dancers, and musicians to explore the rich beauty and the painful ache of the present and the past.

Literature

Jamaicans are storytellers. Their literature, like its West African roots, has a strong oral tradition. Enslaved Africans carried stories and fables with them, sharing them with each other and passing them down to their children. One legendary folk character is the West African spider Anansi. Anansi is a trickster and a hero. He is clever, but he can also be outsmarted. Anansi is sometimes greedy and selfish, but he is also inspiring and magical. Early Jamaican Anansi stories were adapted to reflect the experience of slavery. Sometimes Anansi was a conqueror, and sometimes he was punished and humiliated. But Anansi was never down for long, and there was always another tale to tell.

Jamaicans also tell ghost stories, called "duppy" stories. The Maroons adapted the word *duppy* from the Taino, and the tales blend elements from African and Taino cultures. Duppies are restless wanderers. Good duppies come to people in their sleep and give them advice, while bad duppies bring curses. It is said that it is possible to chase a duppy away by throwing sea salt on it. Duppies are common in children's literature, such as in the 2014 award-winning play, "Three Little Birds."

Crick crack storytelling is another popular African literary form adopted in Jamaica. It includes a call-and-response technique between the storyteller and the audience. As the storyteller moves through a story, he or she will stop and call out "Crick?" and the audience responds "Crack!"

Louise Bennett-Coverley, known as Miss Lou, was Jamaica's most beloved storyteller, performer, actor, and poet. Miss Lou believed that artists should express themselves in the native Jamaican language in order to encourage people to value their heritage and identity. In 1938, Miss Lou wrote poetry for Jamaica's major newspaper and later won a scholarship to attend the Royal Academy of Dramatic Art in London. Soon after arriving in the United Kingdom, she starred in her own television show. When she returned home, she became more and more interested in her native culture and speech and decided to write and perform only in the Jamaican language. Miss Lou's work was lively and playful.

Louise Bennett-Coverley became a member of Jamaica's Order of Merit, the nation's highest honor for artists, in 2001.

Another prominent literary figure was poet and novelist Claude McKay. McKay moved to New York as a young man and became an important figure in the Harlem Renaissance, a flowering of African American culture in the 1920s and 1930s. In much of his work, McKay dealt with issues of black identity.

Younger writers who have achieved acclaim include novelist Kerry Young, who often writes about Jamaica's Chinese community. Another novelist, Colin Channer, has been called "Bob Marley with a pen," because he explores spiritual and social issues in Jamaica.

Claude McKay began writing poetry at age ten and published his first book of poems at age twenty-two.

Edna Manley began creating deeply expressive sculpture in the 1920s and 1930s.

Art

The earliest Jamaican art was Taino sculpture and cave paintings. In the centuries after colonization, when most of the population was enslaved, little visual art was done on the island. Occasionally, a European artist painted portraits of governors, or landscapes with stately colonial mansions.

In the 1930s, new unions and political parties were energizing Jamaicans throughout society, including a group of professional artists. The best known of these artists was Edna Manley, the wife of the leader of the People's National Party. She was frustrated by the colonial culture that choked society. She accompanied a group of artists into a meeting of board members of the Institute of Jamaica, the country's main museum of art and culture. The leader of the group demanded, "Gentlemen, we have come to tell you to tear down these pictures and let Jamaican paintings take their place." Not long after, the institute began displaying the work of Jamaican artists. Eventually, Manley helped estab-

Ebony Patterson's work *Leopard Lily in the Forest* was displayed in an art show in Florida in 2013.

lish what is now called the Edna Manley College of the Visual and Performing Arts in Kingston. Besides being an advocate for Jamaican artists, Edna Manley was one of the country's finest sculptors. Her dramatic bronze sculptures and mahogany wood carvings can be found in museums, galleries, and public spaces.

Many artists benefited from the change at the institute. These include John Dunkley, who painted eerie tropical plants and menacing-looking animals; David Pottinger, who depicted the gloominess and poverty of Kingston shanty-towns; Albert Huie who created dreamy paintings of rural landscapes; and Mallica Reynolds, sometimes known as Kapo, who often painted religious scenes.

Young artists today continue the tradition of interpreting Jamaican life both in its glory and in its grief. The work of

Ebony Patterson has been exhibited in Jamaica, the United States, and beyond. She mixes painting, drawing, collage, video, and other media to explore themes such as young Jamaicans' concepts of beauty and views of themselves.

Get Up, Stand Up

Over the centuries, Jamaican music has typically been based on African rhythms, drums and other percussion instruments, tambourines, horns, and choral chanting and singing. In the early 1900s, a uniquely Jamaican music form called mento spread throughout the country. It was a combination of African and Spanish rhythms and English folk music. A mento band consisted of singers, guitars, banjos, shakers made from dried gourds, and a rumba box, also known as a handmade thumb piano. Mento music remained the most popular Jamaican music until the 1950s when Jamaican musicians started to combine mento with Rasta drumming, creating music called ska. The music was so exciting that Prime Minister Edward Seaga went to New York to promote the ska musicians, and

Artist and Preacher

Mallica Reynolds, usually known as Kapo, was born in a small town in southeastern Jamaica. As a teenager, he began having what he said were religious visions. He became a preacher, and eventually established a Zion Revival church in Trench Town, a poor neighborhood in Kingston. It is said that Kapo continued to have visions, which he interpreted by painting Bible scenes.

Later, he also painted the people of Trench Town, tropical landscapes, and his church. One of his important paintings is called Black Christ by the Sea of Galilee, which shows a black Christ reading to his followers. Kapo's work has been displayed at the National Gallery of Jamaica, and he is treasured today as one of Jamaica's most important cultural figures.

soon Americans, Canadians, and Europeans started listening to the new sounds coming from Jamaica.

In some Kingston neighborhoods, music producers set up massive speakers and boomed ska and other music into the streets. Other people set up different speakers nearby and the thunderous sounds competed with each other, while people danced in the streets. These events were called bashments. The new music scene reflected the times—a country newly independent and full of hope for prosperity and change.

Ska music led to reggae. Reggae was first performed by Rastas, who added more drumming, rock, and brass instruments to ska

Jimmy Cliff starred in the 1972 film *The Harder They Come* and performed many songs in the film. The soundtrack helped popularize reggae around the world.

and sang about spirituality and social change. Reggae musicians, such as Peter Tosh, Bunny Wailer, Marcia Griffiths, Jimmy Cliff, and Bob Marley, rose to stardom. Bob Marley's songs such as "One Love," "Get Up, Stand Up," and "Redemption Song" were about Jamaica and about his faith. He became the first reggae musician to spread the message of Rastafarianism around the world. Many later reggae musicians used their lyrics to express fury at the crime and poverty in Jamaica's cities. The music coming out of Kingston got louder and angrier.

Over the years, Jamaican musicians have continued to innovate. Influenced by African traditions of storytelling, chanting, and driving drumbeats, Jamaican DJs and performing artists were among the first people to perform dancehall music, dub, hip-hop, and rap. Today, Jamaican musicians such as Shaggy, Beenie Man, and Sean Paul have followings around the world.

Bob Marley, who died in 1981, is the best-selling Jamaican musician of all time. He has sold 75 million records worldwide.

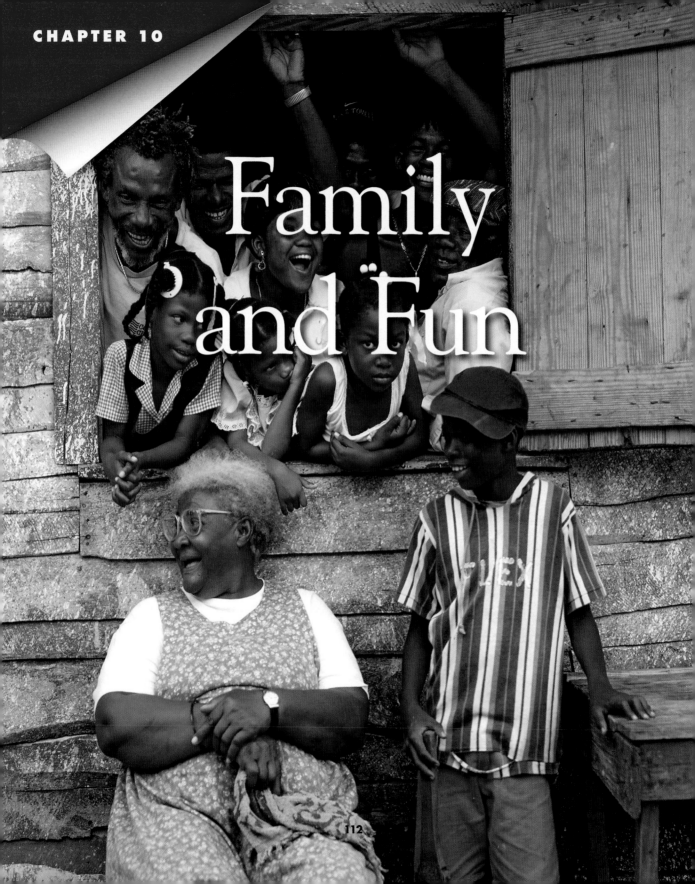

CHAPTER 10

Family and Fun

JAMAICANS ARE CLOSE TO THEIR FAMILIES. AUNTS, uncles, cousins, grandparents, and other extended family members share a strong bond. Extended families participate in raising the children. Older siblings are taught to care for their younger siblings. Children are expected to do chores around the house. Most Jamaicans share traditional family values, such as respecting elders, having good manners, looking after family in times of need, and caring for one another's children. The emotional bond between parents and their children is exceptionally strong.

Opposite: **A Jamaican grandmother enjoys time with her family.**

To Foreign Lands

Many Jamaican professionals such as doctors, lawyers, scientists, and teachers have migrated to Great Britain, the United States, Canada, and other places where they can earn a better income. Some nonprofessional workers also move away to find work and better provide for their families. In some families, the mother moves to Kingston or out of the country. Her children typically stay behind and are cared for by her sister, mother, or another family member. The mother sends money, called remittances, home to support her family and to send her children to private school.

It is estimated that nearly one million Jamaicans receive remittances from family members living abroad. The combined remittances equal the income Jamaicans earn from the tourism industry. Many Jamaicans also ship clothing, shoes, toys, books, and food back home to their family members.

Most Jamaicans who move abroad settle into Jamaican communities in their new countries, and bring Jamaican

A Jamaican boy in New York City prepares to become a U.S. citizen. About 660,000 people born in Jamaica are now living in the United States.

Getting Married

In the past, Jamaican women typically got married at around age eighteen. Now, many do not marry until their late twenties or early thirties. Jamaican weddings resemble British and American weddings, but there is one unusual custom. Before the ceremony, the bride walks down a neighborhood street lined with neighbors, friends, and family. If they do not think she is looking her absolute best, they tell her and she has to go back home and improve her style. After the ceremony, everyone gathers for a feast, music, and dancing. A typical wedding menu is curried goat and rice, beans, salad, punch, champagne, and a dark fruitcake that has been soaked in rum for a year. The festivities last until dawn and anyone, friend or stranger, who happens by is welcome to come in and celebrate.

foods, music, dance, and celebrations to their adopted lands. Well-known Jamaican Americans include Hall of Fame basketball player Patrick Ewing; baseball coach Chili Davis; Grammy Award–winning musicians and singers Sean Paul, Shaggy, and Harry Belafonte; poet Claude McKay; and former U.S. secretary of state Colin Powell.

Food and Drink

Many Jamaican families gather for a big Sunday dinner. Jamaicans eat well and enjoy a healthy diet. Much of their food is fresh and locally grown and nearly everyone shops at the local outdoor farmers' markets when they can. The cuisine is a mix of foods and spices from around the world.

It shows influences from Africa, Europe, India, the Middle East, and China. Everyday favorites include curried goat and rice (Indian); meat pies called patties (British); pumpkin stew (African); bammy, a fried bread made from the cassava root (Taino); and escovitch, a spicy pickled fish (Jewish). A common breakfast is *ackee*, the national fruit, mixed with salt fish. When ackee is prepared it looks like scrambled eggs.

Jamaica's most famous dish is jerk. Jerk is a mixture of sweet and hot spices such as allspice, ginger, and hot peppers. The jerk mix is rubbed on chicken or pork, and then the meat is slow roasted over a wood fire. The usual fire pit is a steel barrel cut in half. Jerk stands are everywhere in Jamaica, and many chefs claim to have a "secret ingredient."

A chef cooks jerk chicken in Port Antonio. *Jerk* comes from a Quechua word meaning "dried meat."

Blue Drawers

Traditionally, this tasty boiled pudding treat is wrapped in banana leaves for cooking, but it is fine to substitute aluminum foil and some string. Have an adult help you with this recipe.

Ingredients

2 cups cornmeal

½ teaspoon salt

¾ cup brown sugar

½ teaspoon grated nutmeg

½ teaspoon cinnamon powder

¼ cup raisins

¼ cup grated coconut

1½ cups coconut milk

1 teaspoon vanilla

Aluminum foil

String

Directions

Fill a soup pot with water and bring it to a boil. Set out 6 pieces of aluminum foil, each about 10 inches square. Mix all the dry ingredients, raisins, and grated coconut together in a large bowl. Add the coconut milk and vanilla, and mix well. Spoon about ⅓ cup of mixture onto a sheet of foil. Fold in the sides of the foil to keep the batter from spilling out. Make sure the foil overlaps thoroughly so it is waterproof. Wrap the string in both directions around the bundle like ribbon on a package. Tie the ends securely. Repeat until all the pieces of foil are filled with batter.

Drop the little packages into the boiling water. There should be enough water to cover them completely. Turn the heat down, and simmer for about an hour. Carefully remove the packages from the water. When they are cool enough to touch, take off the foil and *nyam* (eat)!

Fried or boiled plantains are a common side dish in Jamaica.

Other common foods in Jamaica include plantains (a banana that must be cooked to be eaten), purple star apples, breadfruit, yams, gungo peas, callaloo (a leafy green vegetable eaten at any meal), ugli fruit (oddly shaped and bumpy but delicious), and corn pone. A favorite dessert is a cornmeal and coconut pudding called blue drawers.

Jamaica has many different and flavorful beverages. Many fruit concoctions quench thirst and are made from fresh ingredients. Sorrel drink is made from a leafy green plant, mixed with ginger, sugar, and water. It is often drunk at Christmas and is sometimes used as a folk remedy for a variety of ailments. Soursop is made by mixing the berries of the soursop tree with nutmeg and milk. Jamaicans make ginger beer with ginger, sugar, water, and lime. Carrot juice goes well with the everyday meal of rice and peas. Other common drinks include coffee, coconut milk, and herb teas.

Sports and Games

Along sidewalks, marketplaces, and parks, Jamaicans of all ages play dominoes. Especially in rural communities, playing dominoes is considered a relaxing way to end the day. On weekends, games last late into the night. Families and friends play at parties, family dinners, picnics, and social and church gatherings.

Jamaica's most popular sports are soccer (called football in Jamaica) and cricket. Boys, girls, and adults play football. They play in parks and fields around the island and on more than 250 football clubs. Games can get very competitive and many young people hope to qualify to play in professional or semiprofessional leagues. Jamaica is often ranked number one

Cricket is a high-scoring game. If the batter, called the striker, hits the ball in the air and it passes out of bounds, six runs are scored. If the ball hits the ground before passing out of bounds, four runs are scored.

in the Caribbean leagues. It is a source of great national pride when the Jamaican women's or men's teams do well in international tournaments. The Jamaican national football teams are named the Reggae Boyz and the Reggae Girlz.

Cricket is a British game that has some similarities to baseball. But unlike baseball, cricket games sometimes go on for days, and teams can rack up hundreds of points in a game. The sport is hugely popular in Jamaica, where there are high school, college, and professional men's and women's teams.

Jamaican athletes have shown exceptional talent in track-and-field events. Sprinter Shelly-Ann Fraser-Pryce won gold medals in the 100m race at both the 2008 and 2012 Olympics, and Veronica Campbell-Brown won gold in the 200m race at the 2004 and 2008 Olympics. But no one has so dominated the Olympics as Usain Bolt, who has been called the "fastest man alive." In the 2008 Olympic Games, Bolt won three gold medals—in the 100m race, the 200m race, and the 4-x-100m relay—and broke three world records. At the 2012 games, he repeated his feat, winning three gold medals again.

Holidays and Festivals

Four of Jamaica's ten national holidays are Christian: Ash Wednesday, Good Friday, Easter, and Christmas. Ash Wednesday is the first day of Lent, a solemn forty-day period leading up to Easter. People often attend church and fast on Ash Wednesday. Many give up meat, alcohol, and sweets for all of Lent. Good Friday is the Friday before Easter. Again, most people attend church and fast. On Easter, Christians attend church. Afterward, they enjoy a large family feast. The highlight is Easter bun and cheese. Schoolchildren have a two-week Easter break and many families spend Easter Monday flying kites and going to the beach.

Christmas is celebrated in Jamaica much the same way as it is in the United States and Canada. People attend church, exchange presents, and spend time with family and friends. Traditional Christmas foods include a smoked ham spiced with pimento, and a pudding made of fruit, sugar, and rum.

Dancers perform at an event celebrating the fiftieth anniversary of Jamaican independence.

Jonkonnu

Jonkonnu, or John Canoe, is a festival that occurs near Christmas. It dates back to the days of slavery and has roots in Africa. Once considered "slave Christmas," Jonkonnu was a day that enslaved people did not have to work. They celebrated with parades, music, and special dances. In the parades, men wore frightening masks and elaborate costumes. Some men played special roles, such as a cow that bucked as it danced; a horse that galloped; a devil who spun, kicked, and snarled; and everyone's favorite, the pitchy patchy, an urchin in rags and feathers who danced crazily in and out of the parade. Today, the largest Jonkonnu celebration is in Kingston, and it remains an important holiday in Jamaica.

Other Jamaican holidays celebrate important moments in history. Emancipation Day celebrates the day that enslaved Jamaicans were freed. Many Jamaicans celebrate Emancipation Day on the night of July 31, despite the fact that the national holiday is August 1. When the Emancipation Act became law in 1834, the former slaves were forced to work without pay until August 1, 1838, before they would be free. As August 1 drew near, the former slaves did not trust that they would actually be free to live their own lives. So just after midnight on July 31, they quietly left the plantations and climbed to the tops of mountains and prayed, waiting to see if freedom would really come. At dawn, learning that they were truly free, the people came down from the hills and went to churches and gave thanks. Today, many Jamaicans hold vigils on July 31, drumming and ringing bells, while in Spanish Town people gather in the town square for a reading of the Emancipation Declaration.

National Heroes Day is celebrated the third Monday in October. It is the end of a week of celebrations called National Heritage Week, during which each parish honors the dead

and stages music, dance, and poetry presentations, flag-raising ceremonies, and exhibits of student accomplishments in

Sprinter Usain Bolt (right) receives an award on National Heroes Day.

National Holidays

New Year's Day	January 1
Ash Wednesday	February or March
Good Friday	March or April
Easter Monday	March or April
Labor Day	May 23
Emancipation Day	August 1
Independence Day	August 6
National Heroes Day	October (third Monday)
Christmas Day	December 25
Boxing Day	December 26

Maroons march through Accompong in celebration of Cudjoe's birthday.

the arts and sciences. On National Heroes Day, citizens are awarded honors for their contribution to the arts and sciences, and for their service to the country. The highest award is National Hero. Only seven people have been named National Heroes: Paul Bogle, George William Gordon, Marcus Garvey, Sir Alexander Bustamante, Norman Manley, Samuel Sharpe, and Queen Nanny of the Maroons.

Jamaica also celebrates many local, regional, and ethnic festivals. Each year on January 4 the Maroons of Accompong begin a three-day celebration honoring the birthday of Cudjoe, the Maroon leader who signed the peace treaty with the British giving escaped slaves their freedom and the right to govern themselves. The ceremony opens with the sound of a traditional horn called an *abeng*. Cudjoe used an abeng to signal the Maroons to gather for a raid. During the ceremony, songs are performed in African languages while drummers and horn players attempt to work dancers into a state of *myal*, a spiritual trance. The ceremony also includes a feast. The centerpiece is a roasted black male pig, raised especially for the event. Vendors and craftspeople sell their traditional arts and crafts, such as bamboo baskets and African clay cooking pots.

One of the largest Jamaican festivals was established in 1990 by a teacher called Sister P, who ran an African-centered school near the John Crow Mountains. One year she produced a program to display her students' talents, and thirty people

During the Accompong Maroon festival, people gather under an ancient mango called the Kindah Tree.

attended. Over the years, this program turned into a major heritage festival attracting thousands of people. The festival is named Fi Wi Sinting, which is Jamaican for "For us, our something." It includes mento, reggae, myal dancers, African call-and-response singing, as well as traditional arts and crafts. There is a Jonkonnu parade, and many other uniquely Jamaican performances. The festival ends with people making offerings to their ancestors and placing the offerings on a bamboo raft that floats downriver and out into the Caribbean Sea.

Young people perform at a festival in Kingston.

To the Future

The history of Jamaica is filled with suffering, but now, just decades after independence, the people of Jamaica are making progress toward a better future. Tourism is expanding, providing more jobs. People across Jamaican society are coming together and pressuring government agencies to fight drug use and trade, crime, and unemployment in the cities. The government is also responding to the needs of the people by expanding programs to improve education, develop rural areas, and expand markets for agricultural and manufactured goods. Environmentalists are increasing awareness of the need to protect Jamaica's precious natural resources. There is every reason to believe Jamaicans will overcome their current challenges, since they have suffered far worse. The country is endowed with exceptional riches, the greatest of which is its people who savor life with resourcefulness and humor.

About 28 percent of Jamaicans are under fifteen years old.

Timeline

JAMAICAN HISTORY		WORLD HISTORY	
		ca. 2500 BCE	The Egyptians build the pyramids and the Sphinx in Giza.
		ca. 563 BCE	The Buddha is born in India.
		313 CE	The Roman emperor Constantine legalizes Christianity.
Tainos settle in Jamaica.	ca. 600 CE	610	The Prophet Muhammad begins preaching a new religion called Islam.
		1054	The Eastern (Orthodox) and Western (Roman Catholic) Churches break apart.
		1095	The Crusades begin.
		1215	King John seals the Magna Carta.
		1300s	The Renaissance begins in Italy.
		1347	The plague sweeps through Europe.
		1453	Ottoman Turks capture Constantinople, conquering the Byzantine Empire.
Christopher Columbus lands in Discovery Bay, Jamaica.	1494	1492	Columbus arrives in North America.
		1500s	Reformers break away from the Catholic Church, and Protestantism is born.
Spain begins colonizing Jamaica.	1510		
The British seize control of Jamaica.	1655		
Spain cedes Jamaica to Great Britain.	1670		
The First Maroon War begins.	1690		
An earthquake destroys Port Royal.	1692		
The Leeward Maroons sign a peace treaty with the British.	1739		
		1776	The U.S. Declaration of Independence is signed.
		1789	The French Revolution begins.
Samuel Sharpe leads the Christmas Rebellion.	1831		

Enslaved people in Jamaica are completely emancipated.	**1838**		
The white rulers of Jamaica execute hundreds of black Jamaicans following the Morant Bay Rebellion.	**1865**	**1865**	The American Civil War ends.
Jamaica becomes a crown colony.	**1866**	**1879**	The first practical lightbulb is invented.
An earthquake destroys Kingston.	**1907**		
Marcus Garvey establishes the Universal Negro Improvement Association.	**1914**	**1914**	World War I begins.
		1917	The Bolshevik Revolution brings communism to Russia.
		1929	A worldwide economic depression begins.
		1939	World War II begins.
Alexander Bustamante founds the Jamaica Labor Party.	**1943**		
All adults in Jamaica are given the right to vote.	**1944**	**1945**	World War II ends.
Jamaica becomes independent; Alexander Bustamante becomes its first prime minister.	**1962**	**1969**	Humans land on the Moon.
The People's National Party wins national elections; Michael Manley becomes prime minister.	**1972**	**1975**	The Vietnam War ends.
About eight hundred people are killed in political violence during the national elections.	**1980**	**1989**	The Berlin Wall is torn down as communism crumbles in Eastern Europe.
		1991	The Soviet Union breaks into separate states.
		2001	Terrorists attack the World Trade Center in New York City and the Pentagon near Washington, D.C.
Portia Simpson Miller becomes Jamaica's first female prime minister.	**2006**	**2004**	A tsunami in the Indian Ocean destroys coastlines in Africa, India, and Southeast Asia.
		2008	The United States elects its first African American president.

Fast Facts

Official name: Jamaica

Capital: Kingston

Date of independence: August 6, 1962

Official language: English

Kingston

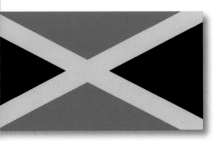

National flag

National anthem: "Jamaica, Land We Love"

Government: Constitutional parliamentary democracy

Head of state: British monarch

Head of government: Prime minister

Area of country: 4,243 square miles (10,990 sq km)

Highest elevation: Blue Mountain Peak, 7,402 feet (2,256 m)

Lowest elevation: Sea level, along the coasts

Longest river: Rio Minho, 58 miles (93 km)

Average high temperature: In Kingston, 87°F (30°C) in January; 91°F (33°C) in July

Average low temperature: In Kingston, 70°F (21°C) in January, 76°F (24°C) in July

Average annual precipitation: In Kingston, 32 inches (81 cm)

Blue Mountains

Montego Bay

National population (2014 est.):	2,930,050	
Population of major cities (2011 est.):	Kingston	666,041
	Portmore	182,153
	Spanish Town	147,152
	Montego Bay	110,115
	May Pen	61,548

Landmarks:

▶ *Blue and John Crow Mountains National Park*, Portland Parish

▶ *Bob Marley Museum*, Kingston

▶ *Dunns River Falls*, Ocho Rios

▶ *Montego Bay Marine Park*, Montego Bay

▶ *Museums of History and Ethnography*, Kingston

Economy: Jamaica mines bauxite, limestone, gypsum, silica, and marble. Major agricultural products include bananas, sugar, citrus fruit, and coffee. Tourism is the nation's largest industry. The country attracts two million visitors every year.

Currency: The Jamaican dollar. In 2014, J$113 equaled US$1.

System of weights and measures: Metric system

Literacy rate (2012): 88%

Currency

Wha' gwan?	What's going on?
All fruits ripe.	Everything is good/appealing.
Cool runnings.	Have a safe trip.
Likkle more.	See you later.
Walk good.	Good-bye, be safe.

Student

Bob Marley

Prominent Jamaicans:

Louise Bennett-Coverley	(1919–2006)
Storyteller, actor, and poet	
Usain Bolt	(1986–)
Olympic champion sprinter	
Alexander Bustamante	(1884–1977)
Labor leader and first prime minister	
Marcus Garvey	(1887–1940)
Black nationalist leader	
Edna Manley	(1900–1987)
Sculptor and supporter of Jamaican artists	
Bob Marley	(1945–1981)
Reggae musician	
Queen Nanny of the Maroons	(ca. 1685–?)
Maroon leader of ex-slaves	
Samuel Sharpe	(1801–1832)
Minister who led slave uprising	

To Find Out More

Books

- Cantor, George. *Usain Bolt.* Detroit: Lucent Books, 2011.

- Capek, Michael. *Jamaica.* Minneapolis: Lerner, 2010.

- Haskins, Jim. *One Love, One Heart: A History of Reggae.* New York: Hyperion, 2002.

- Yancey, Diane. *Piracy on the High Seas.* Detroit: Lucent Books, 2012.

Music

- Aitken, Laurel. *Calypso Rock & Roll: Early Mento Recordings.* Glendale, CA: Cobraside, 2012.

- Dekker, Desmond. *King of Ska.* London: Secret Recordings, 2011.

- Marley, Bob. *Legend: The Best of Bob Marley and the Wailers.* New York: Island Records, 2002.

- Shaggy. *Best of Shaggy: The Boombastic Collection.* Santa Monica, CA: Hip-O Records, 2008.

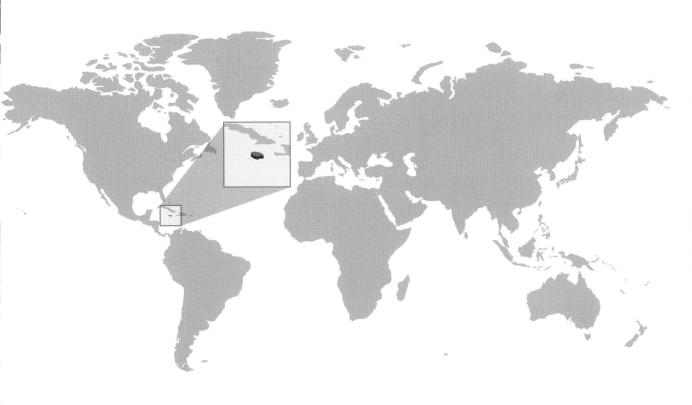

▶ Visit this Scholastic Web site for more information on Jamaica:
www.factsfornow.scholastic.com
Enter the keyword Jamaica

Index

Page numbers in *italics* indicate illustrations.

mangrove trees, 36–37, *37*
mountains, 9
pimento trees, 10–11, 12, 15, 17
rain forests, 22
trees, 10–11, 12, 14, 15, *16*, 17,
    36–37, *36*, *37*, *125*
wildflowers, 36, *36*
political parties, 53, 54, 55, 56–57,
    63, 64
pollution, 79
population, 27, 40, 44, 68, 81, 88,
    89, 90
Port Antonio, *116*
Port Maria, 47
Portmore, 27, 89
Port Royal, *41*, 43, 44, *44*, 68
Pottinger, David, 108
poverty, 59, 89–90, 111
Powell, Colin, 115
prime ministers, 55, *55*, 57, *57*, 62–63,
    66, *66*, 85, 109–110, 133
Privy Council, 63, 69
Protestantism, 96–98, *98*
proverbs, 88

Q
Queen Nanny (Maroon leader), 48,
    48, 124, 133

R
railroads, 53
rain forests, 22
Rastafarianism, 99–101, *100*, 111
rats, 31
recipe, 117, *117*
Reggae Boyz (football team), 120
Reggae Girlz (football team), 120
reggae music, 110–111, *110*, *111*, 126
religion
    African people, 95
    agriculture and, 93
    art and, *92*, 108

Ash Wednesday, 120
Baptist Church, 96–97
Bobo Shanti group, 101
British colonization and, 83, 95,
    96
Burchell Baptist Church, 27
Catholicism, *82*, 83, 94–95, 95–96,
    96
Chapel of the Red Cross, 27
Christmas holiday, 121
Church of England, 96
Church of God, 96
conversos, 95
Easter holiday, 120–121
Good Friday, 120
Great Revival movement, 97
holidays, 84, 120–121, 123
Judaism, 83–84, *94*, 95
Kumina, 98, 99
Obeah, 48, 101, *101*
parishes, 69
Protestantism, 96–98, *98*
Rastafarianism, 99–101, *100*, 111
Revivalism, 98–99, 109
Shaare Shalom Synagogue, *94*,
    95, *95*
slavery and, 97
Spanish colonization and, 94
Spanish Inquisition, 94
Spanish Town Cathedral, 27, *82*,
    82, 94
Taino people, *92*, 93, 94
United Congregation of Israelites,
    95
zemis (spirit idols), *92*, 93
remittances, 114
reptilian life, 31, 34–35, *34*, *35*
Revivalism, 98–99, 109
Reynolds, Mallica "Kapo," 108, 109
Rio Cobre, 24
Rio Grande River, 20
Rio Minho, 21, 24

roadways, 53, 59
rural areas, 90, 127

S
Sam Sharpe Square, 27, *27*
Seacole, Mary, 51, *51*
Seaford Town, 96
Seaga, Edward, 59, 85, 109
sea turtles, 34, *34*
Second Maroon War, 48–49
sedimentary rock, 22
Selassie, Haile, I, 99–100
Senate, 64
Sereba, Kouame, *104*
service industries, 77, *77*, 90
Sevilla la Nueva colony, 40
Shaare Shalom Synagogue, *94*, 95, *95*
Shaggy, 115
shantytowns, 89–90, 108
Sharpe, Samuel, 27, 50, 76, 124, 133
Sherlock, Hugh Braham, 67
shipping, *41*, 45, *45*, 78
Sister P, 125–126
ska music, 109–110
Sloane, Hans, 29
snakes, 34
soccer, 119
social media, 79
soursop (beverage), 118
Spanish colonization, 11, 27, 36,
    39–40, *40*, 41, 81, 82, 94
Spanish Inquisition, 94
Spanish Town. *See also* cities.
    architecture, 27, *27*, 82, *82*
    British colonization and, 41, 42
    as capital, 27, 42
    Chapel of the Red Cross, 27
    Emancipation Day in, 122
    People's Museum of Craft and
        Technology, 27
    political conflict in, 58
    population of, 27, 89

Spanish colonization and, 27, 82, 94
Spanish Town Cathedral, 27, 82, 82, 94
as Villa de la Vega, 27
Speaker of the House, 65
sports, 115, 119–120, *119*, *123*, 133
St. Ann Parish, 9, 17, 99
St. Ann's Bay, 40, 54, 80
storytelling, *102*, *104*
sugarcane, 27, 31, 40, 44–45, 46, *49*, 53, 71
Supreme Court, 69
Syrian people, 85

T
Tacky Falls, 24, 48
Tacky (rebellion leader), 48
Taino people. *See also* people.
    agriculture, 39, 40
    art, 107
    artifacts, *38*
    currency and, 76
    diseases and, 40
    foods, 116
    guaiacum tree and, 36
    language, 82, 85, 104
    Maroons and, 81–82
    Martha Brae, 25
    religion of, *92*, 93, 94
    as settlers, 19, 39
    slavery and, 40
    Spanish colonization and, 39–40, 81
    swallowtail hummingbird and, 30
taxes, 57
television, 105
threatened species, 34, 35
"Three Little Birds" (play), 104
Throne Speech, 64
tourism, 27, 53, 59, 68, 75, 77–79, *78*, 90, 127
towns. *See also* cities; villages.
    agriculture in, 90

employment and, 90
    Falmouth, 59
    names of, 85
    Negril, 23
    Port Antonio, *116*
    Port Maria, 47
    Seaford Town, 96
track-and-field, 120
trade unions, 57, 59
transportation, 23, 53
Trench Town neighborhood, 109
Trianglular Trade, 45–46, *45*
tropical storms, 13–15, *13*, 16, *16*, 26, 53
tsunamis, 44, *44*

U
United Congregation of Israelites, 95
United States, 53, 54, 55, *57*, 59, 72, 74, 97, 106, 108, 110, 113, *114*, 115
Universal Negro Improvement Association, 54

V
villages. *See also* cities; towns.
    agriculture in, 90
    employment and, 90
    Nanny Town, 48
    Villa de la Vega, 27, 40
Voice, The (television show), 79

W
waterfalls, 9, *18*, 24, *24*, 37
West Indies Federation, 55
wetlands, 35
white people, 11, 27, 50–51, 53, 81, 84, 95, 100
wildflowers, 36
wildlife. *See* amphibian life; animal life; insect life; marine life; plant life; reptilian life.
wild pigs, 31, 42, 47

Windward Maroons, 46, 48
women, *11*, 51, *51*, 66, 66, 115, *115*, 120

Y
yellow-billed Amazon parrot, 30
Yom Kippur, 84
Young, Kerry, 106
YS Falls, 24
YS River, 25

Z
zemis (spirit idols), *92*, 93

Meet the Author

RUTH BJORKLUND SPENT HER CHILDHOOD IN RURAL New England, living in a house on a lake where she developed a love of nature and a passion for living near water. She spent summers rowing her small boat and hiking in the nearby woods. When she was twenty, she packed up her belongings and moved to the Pacific Northwest.

Bjorklund graduated from the University of Washington with a degree in comparative literature and later earned a master's degree in library and information science. She worked for several years as a children's and young adult librarian and then began writing books for young people. She has written on a variety of subjects, including endangered animals, medicine, childhood diseases, ancient China, Afghanistan, aikido, Native Americans, immigration, and hydrofracking.

Bjorklund presently lives on Bainbridge Island, a ferry ride away from Seattle, Washington. Wherever and whenever she can, she enjoys sailing, snorkeling, birding, kayaking, fly-fishing, and at the end of the day, a comfortable place to read.

Photo Credits